W9-CEK-098

GRAPHIC SCIENCE

LESSONS IN SCIENCE SAFETY

with MAX AXIOM SUPER SCIENTIST

by Donald B. Lemke and Thomas K. Adamson

illustrated by Tod Smith and Bill Anderson

Consultant:
Dr. Ronald Browne
Associate Professor of Elementary Education
Minnesota State University, Mankato

Capstone press

Mankato, Minnesota

Graphic Library is published by Capstone Press,
1710 Roe Crest Drive, North Mankato, Minnesota 56003.
www.capstonepub.com

Library of Congress Cataloging-in-Publication Data
Lemke, Donald B.
    Lessons in science safety with Max Axiom, super scientist / by Donald B. Lemke and
Thomas K. Adamson; illustrated by Tod Smith and Bill Anderson.
    p. cm.—(Graphic library. Graphic science)
    Includes bibliographical references and index.
    ISBN-13: 978-0-7368-6834-1 (hardcover)
    ISBN-10: 0-7368-6834-8 (hardcover)
    ISBN-13: 978-0-7368-7887-6 (softcover pbk.)
    ISBN-10: 0-7368-7887-4 (softcover pbk.)
    1. Science—Experiments—Safety measures—Juvenile literature. 2. Laboratories Safety
measures—Juvenile literature. I. Adamson, Thomas K., 1970– II. Smith, Tod, ill. III.
Anderson, Bill, 1963– ill. IV. Title. V. Series.
Q182.3.L347 2007
507.8—dc22   2006027996

Summary: In graphic novel format, follows the adventures of Max Axiom as he explains the
    importance of science safety.

Art Director and Designer
Bob Lentz

Cover Artist
Tod Smith

Colorist
Otha Zackariah Edward Lohse

Editor
Christopher L. Harbo

Printed and bound in the United States of America.
052019   002074

TABLE of CONTENTS

SECTION 1

PREPARING FOR THE LAB ------- 4

SECTION 2

WORKING SAFELY ----------------- 8

SECTION 3

HANDLING ACCIDENTS ------------16

SECTION 4

CLEANING UP --------------------- 24

More about Science Safety and Max Axiom....................28–29
Glossary 30
Read More 31
Internet Sites 31
Index... 32

SECTION 1 PREPARING FOR THE LAB

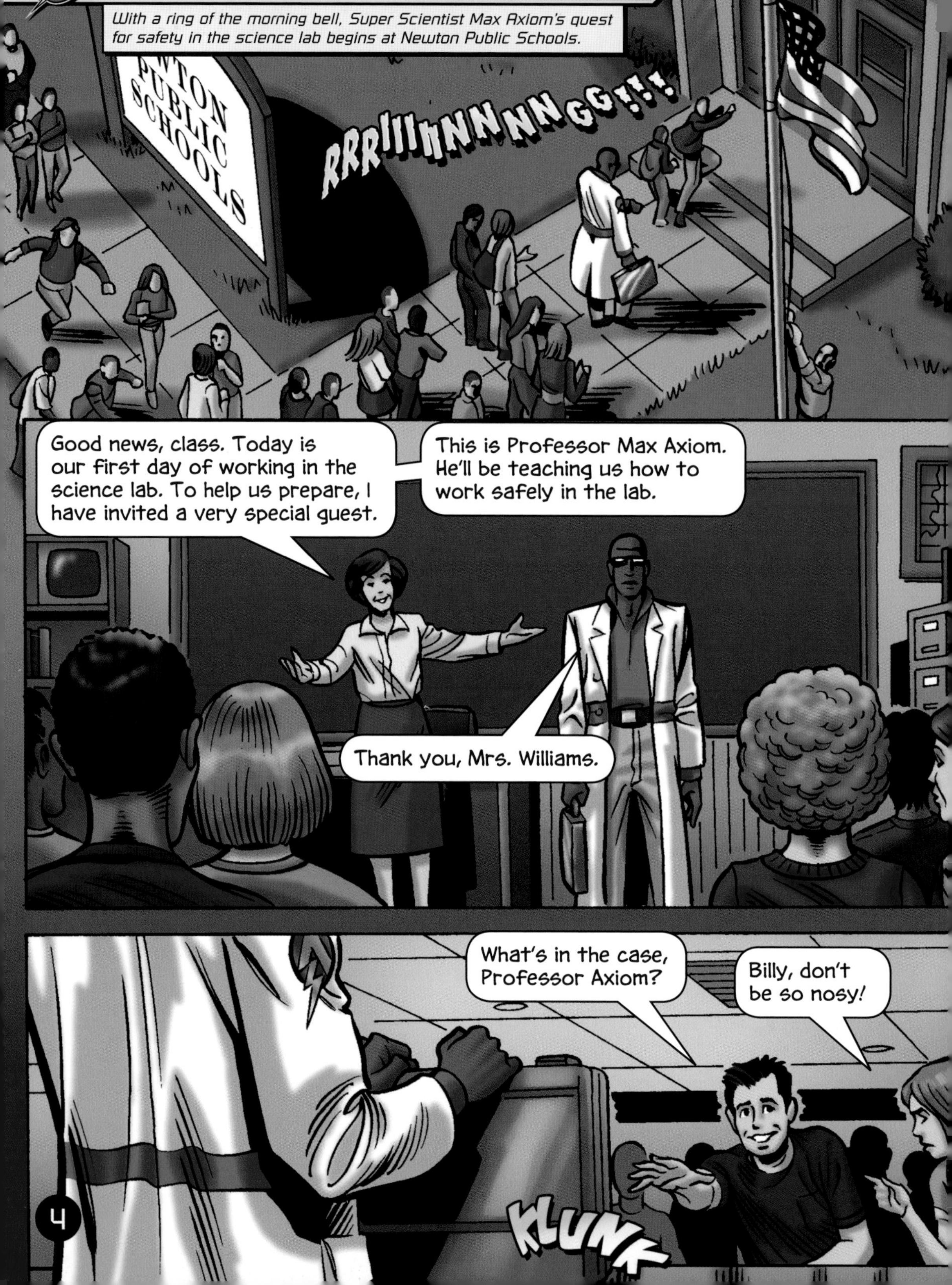
With a ring of the morning bell, Super Scientist Max Axiom's quest for safety in the science lab begins at Newton Public Schools.
WTON PUBLIC SCHOOLS
RRRIIIINNNNNGG!!!
Good news, class. Today is our first day of working in the science lab. To help us prepare, I have invited a very special guest.
This is Professor Max Axiom. He'll be teaching us how to work safely in the lab.
Thank you, Mrs. Williams.
What's in the case, Professor Axiom?
Billy, don't be so nosy!
KLUNK

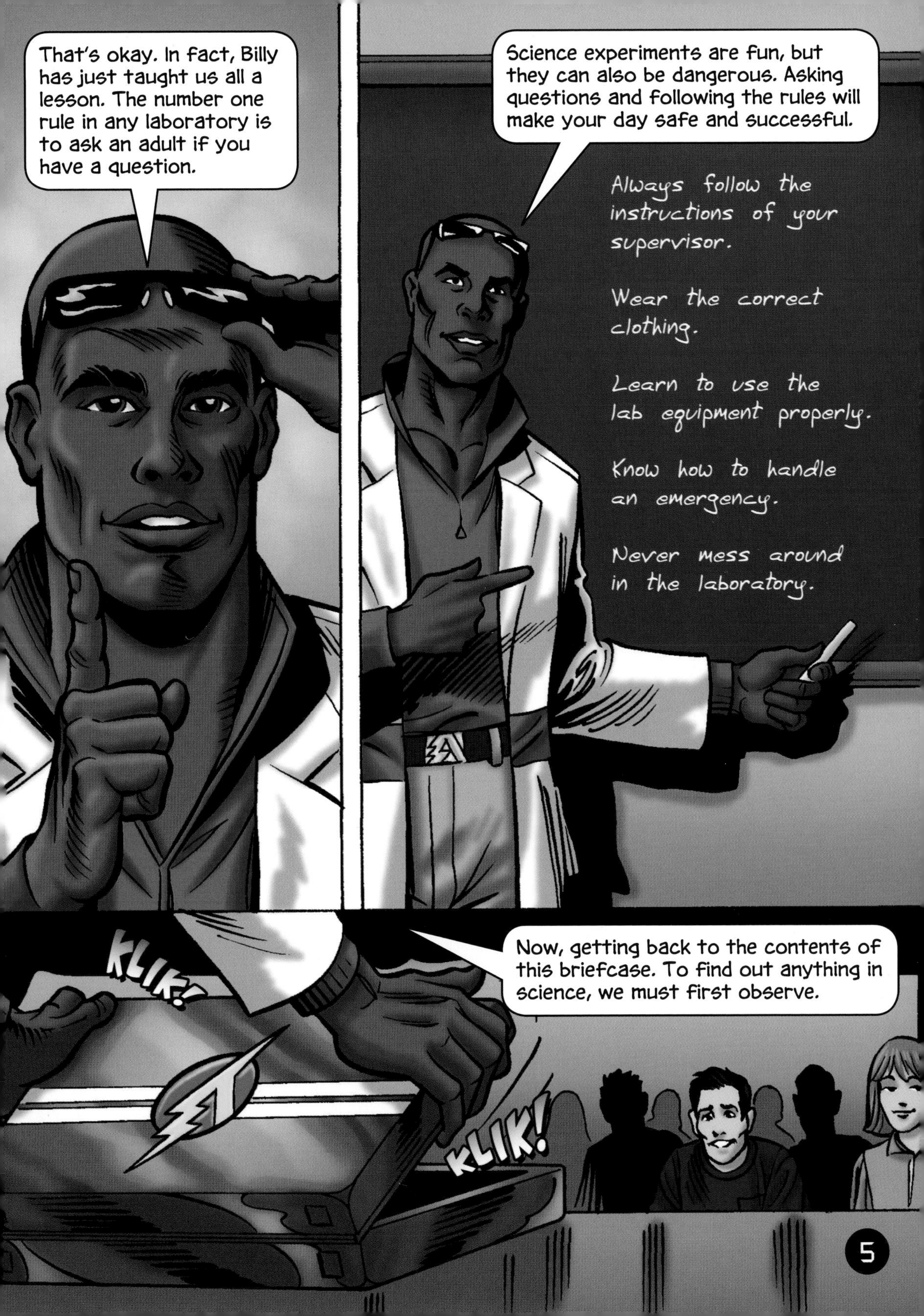

That's okay. In fact, Billy has just taught us all a lesson. The number one rule in any laboratory is to ask an adult if you have a question.
Science experiments are fun, but they can also be dangerous. Asking questions and following the rules will make your day safe and successful.
Always follow the instructions of your supervisor.
Wear the correct clothing.
Learn to use the lab equipment properly.
Know how to handle an emergency.
Never mess around in the laboratory.
KLIK!
Now, getting back to the contents of this briefcase. To find out anything in science, we must first observe.
KLIK!

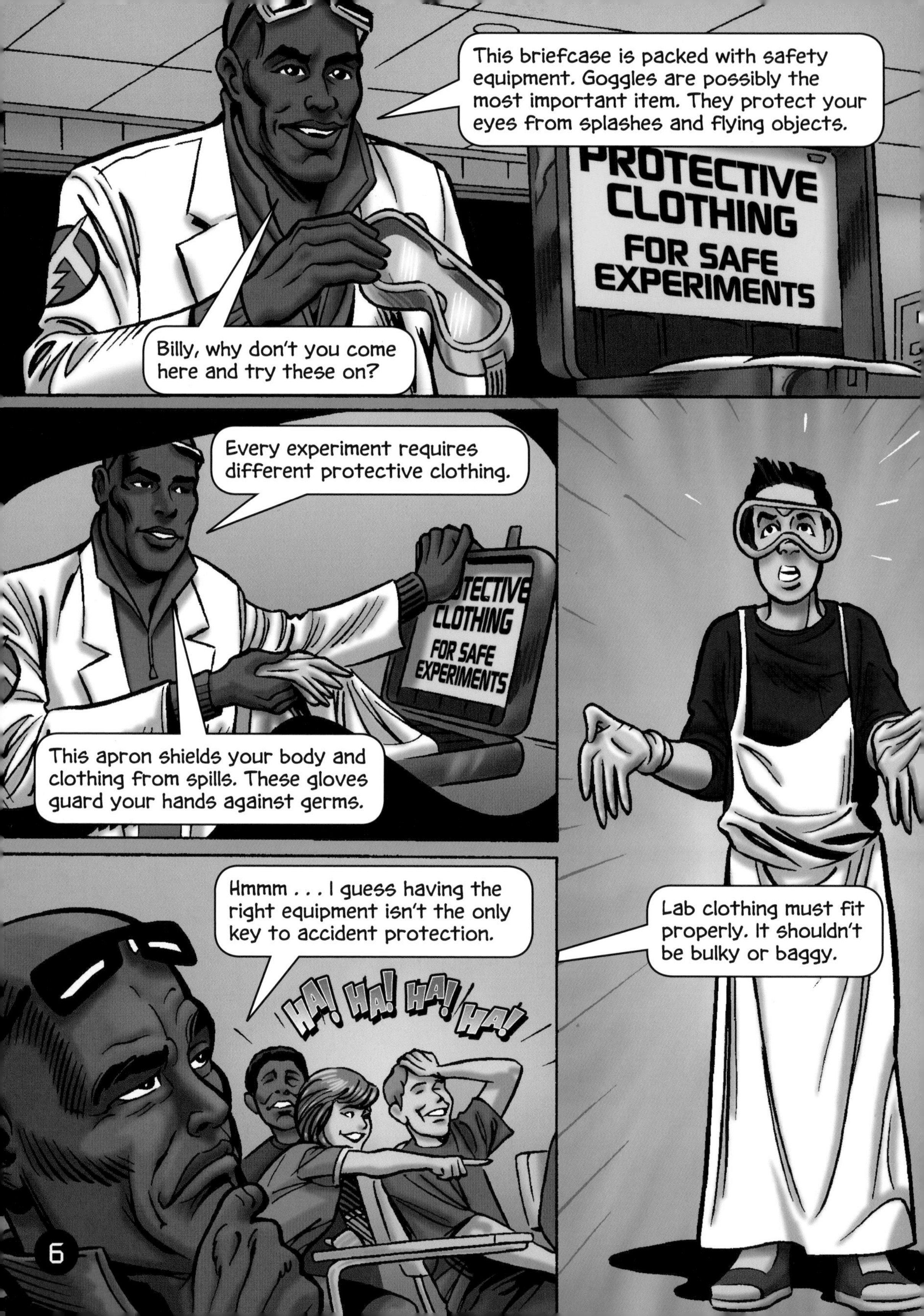
This briefcase is packed with safety equipment. Goggles are possibly the most important item. They protect your eyes from splashes and flying objects.
PROTECTIVE CLOTHING FOR SAFE EXPERIMENTS
Billy, why don't you come here and try these on?
Every experiment requires different protective clothing.
PROTECTIVE CLOTHING FOR SAFE EXPERIMENTS
This apron shields your body and clothing from spills. These gloves guard your hands against germs.
Lab clothing must fit properly. It shouldn't be bulky or baggy.
Hmmm . . . I guess having the right equipment isn't the only key to accident protection.
HA! HA! HA! HA!

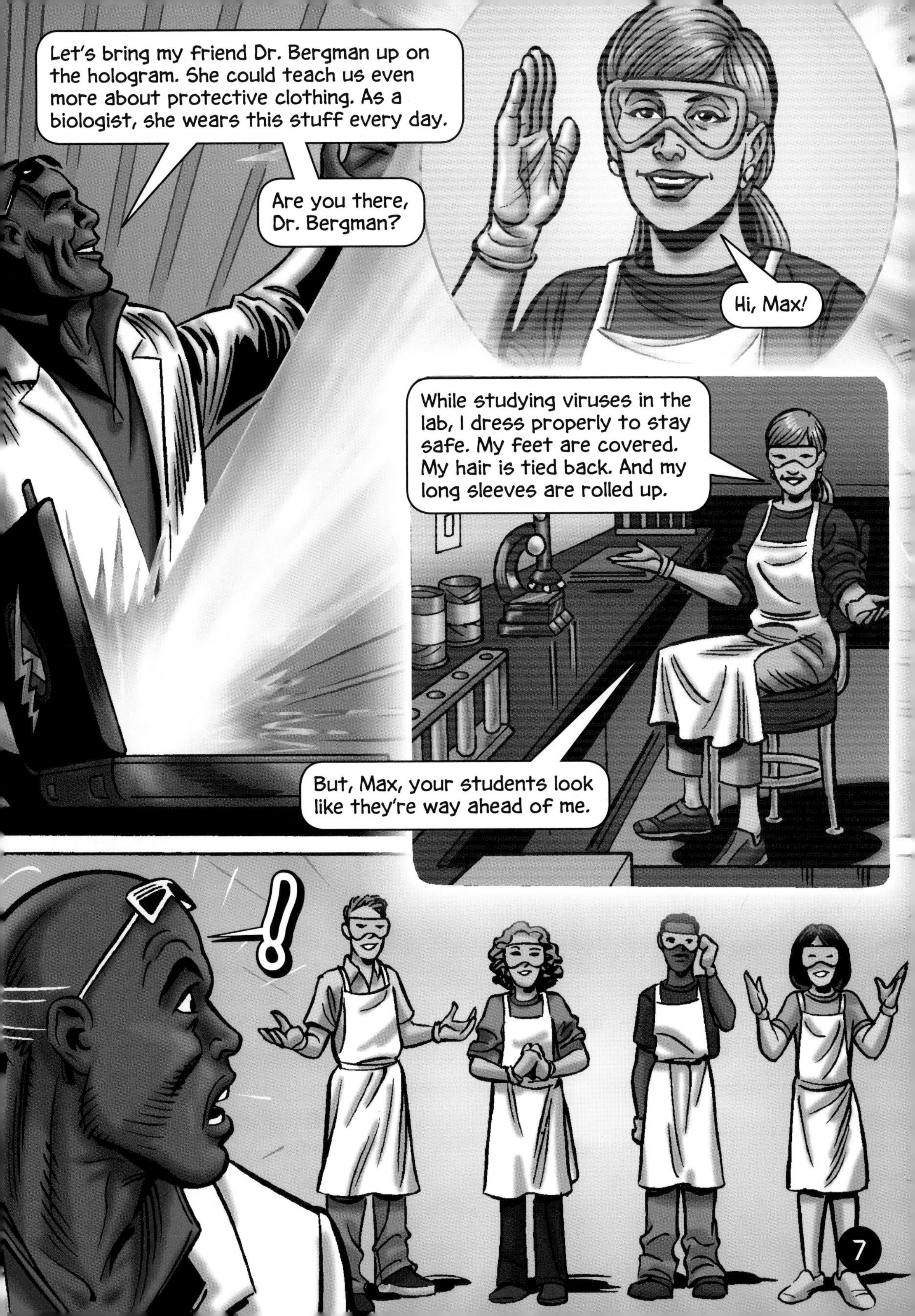

Let's bring my friend Dr. Bergman up on the hologram. She could teach us even more about protective clothing. As a biologist, she wears this stuff every day.
Are you there, Dr. Bergman?
Hi, Max!
While studying viruses in the lab, I dress properly to stay safe. My feet are covered. My hair is tied back. And my long sleeves are rolled up.
But, Max, your students look like they're way ahead of me.
!

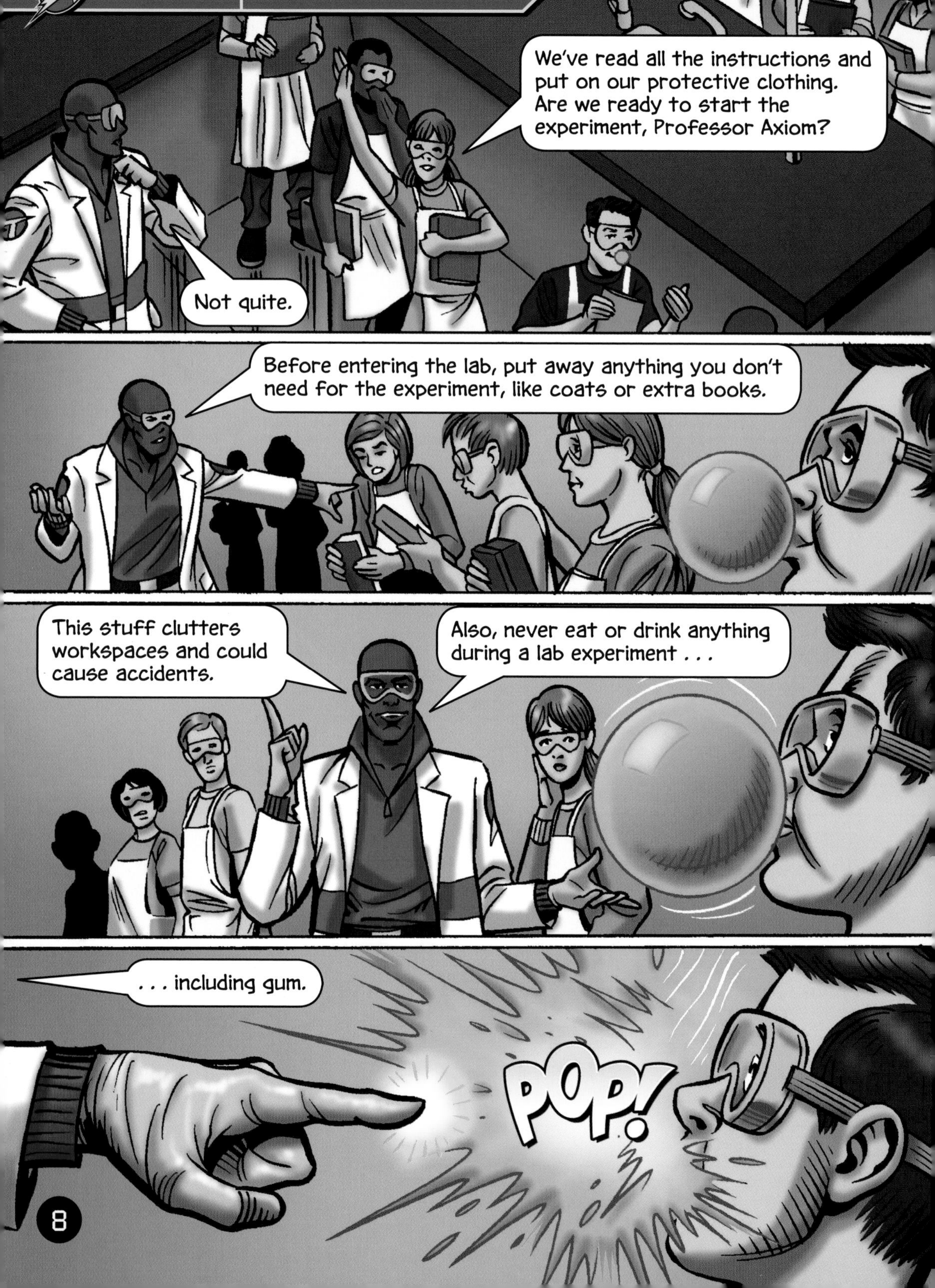
We've read all the instructions and put on our protective clothing. Are we ready to start the experiment, Professor Axiom?
Not quite.
Before entering the lab, put away anything you don't need for the experiment, like coats or extra books.
This stuff clutters workspaces and could cause accidents.
Also, never eat or drink anything during a lab experiment . . .
. . . including gum.
POP!

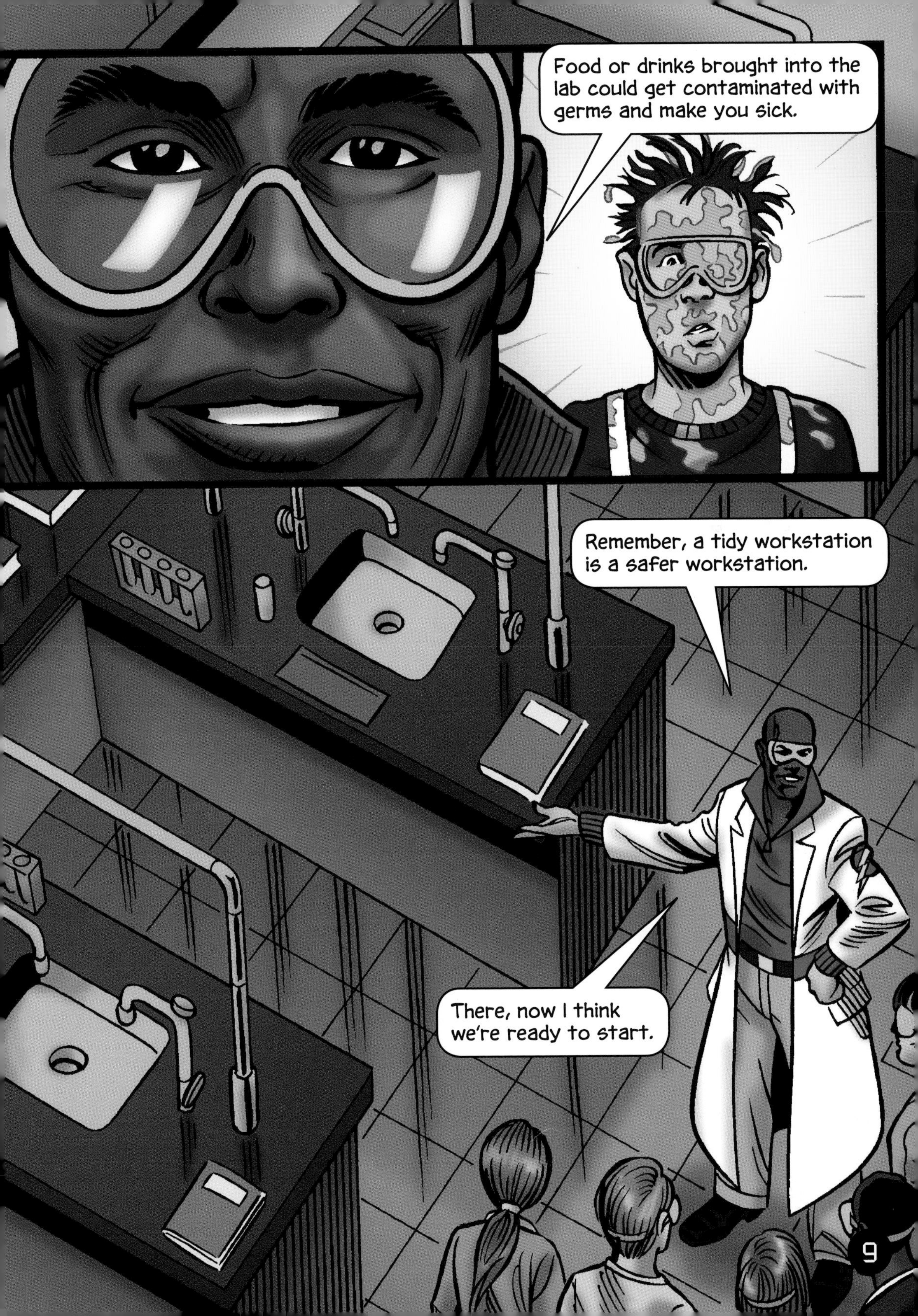

Food or drinks brought into the lab could get contaminated with germs and make you sick.
Remember, a tidy workstation is a safer workstation.
There, now I think we're ready to start.

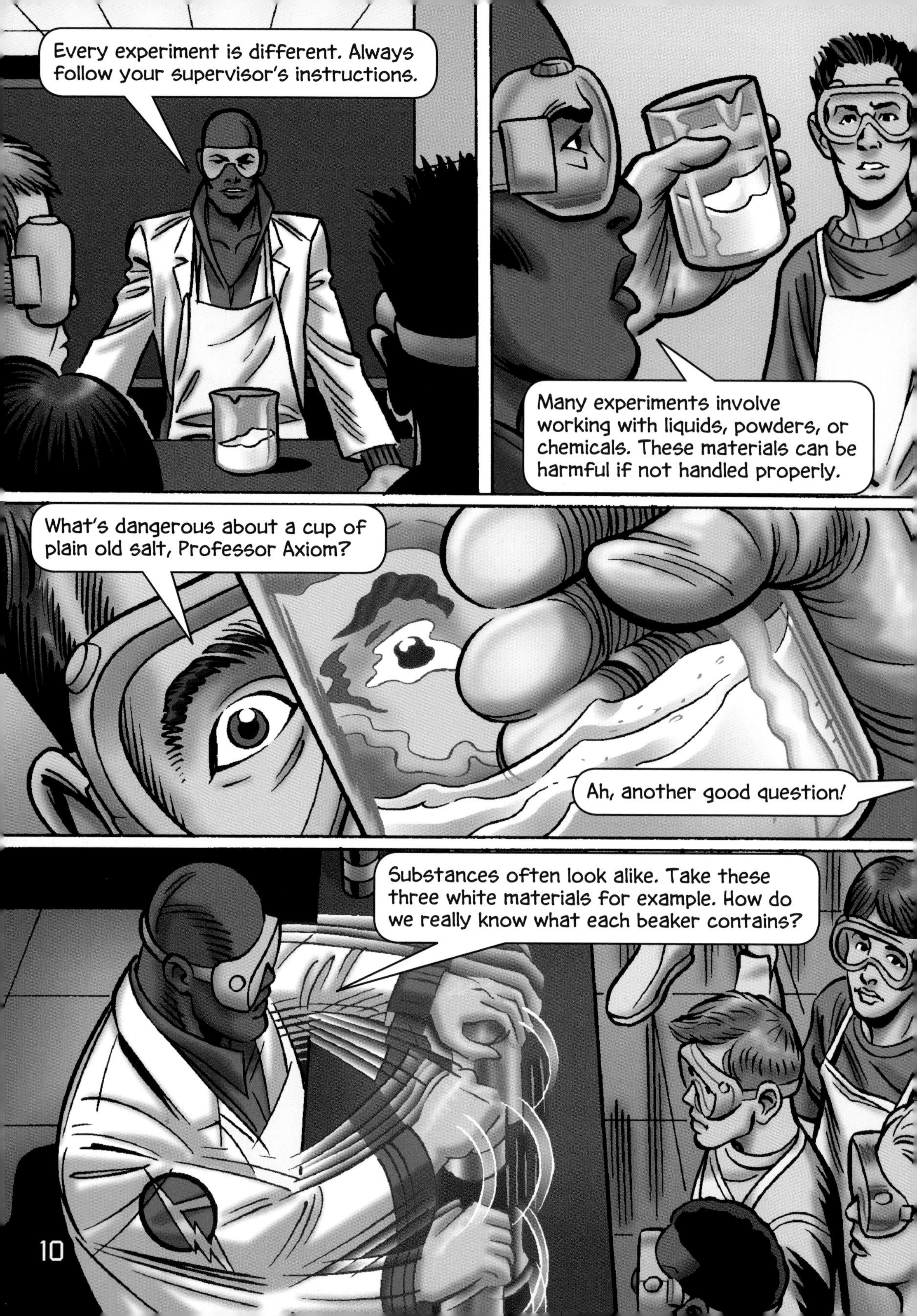
Every experiment is different. Always follow your supervisor's instructions.
Many experiments involve working with liquids, powders, or chemicals. These materials can be harmful if not handled properly.
What's dangerous about a cup of plain old salt, Professor Axiom?
Ah, another good question!
Substances often look alike. Take these three white materials for example. How do we really know what each beaker contains?

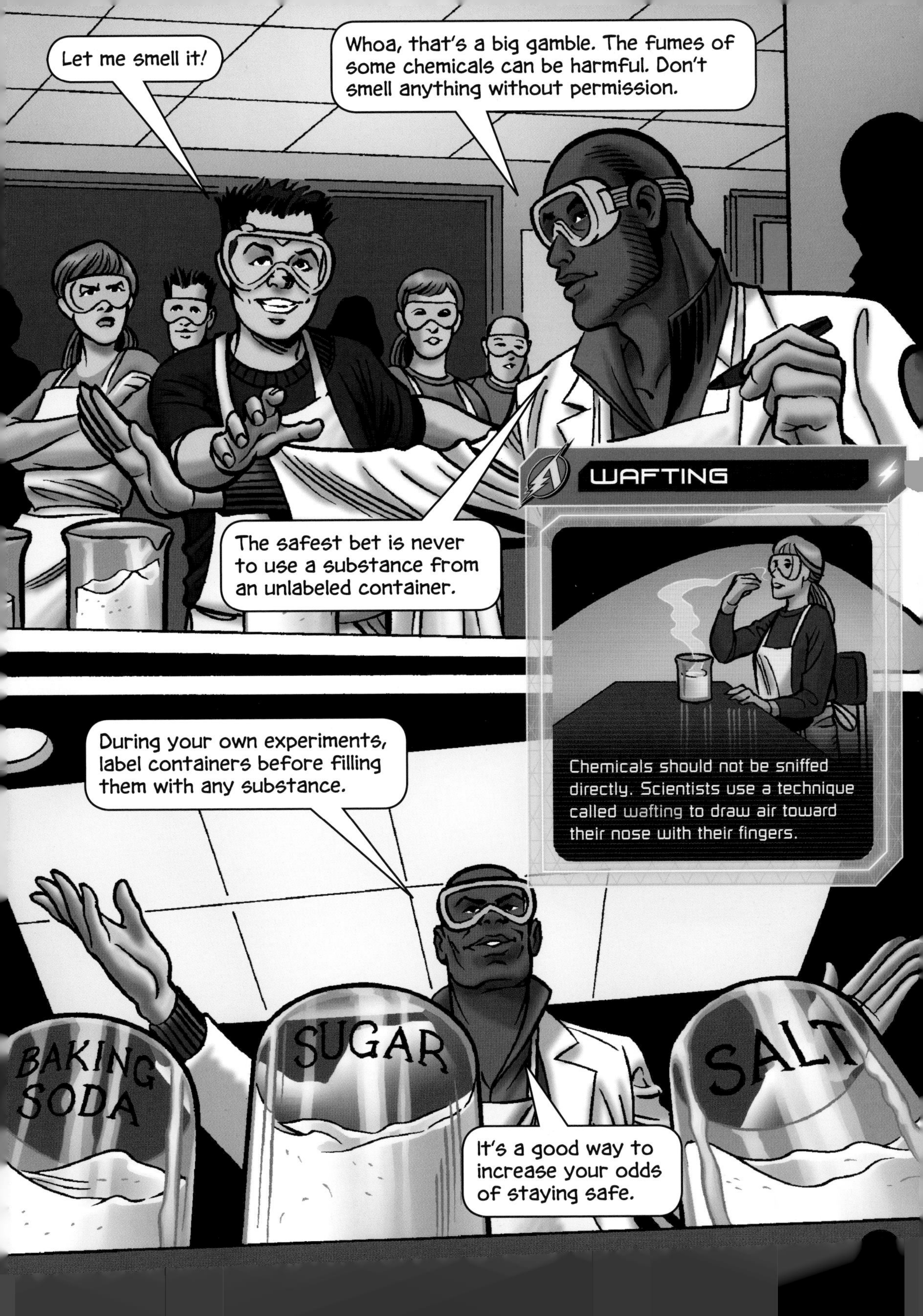
Let me smell it!
Whoa, that's a big gamble. The fumes of some chemicals can be harmful. Don't smell anything without permission.
The safest bet is never to use a substance from an unlabeled container.
WAFTING
Chemicals should not be sniffed directly. Scientists use a technique called wafting to draw air toward their nose with their fingers.
During your own experiments, label containers before filling them with any substance.
BAKING SODA
SUGAR
SALT
It's a good way to increase your odds of staying safe.

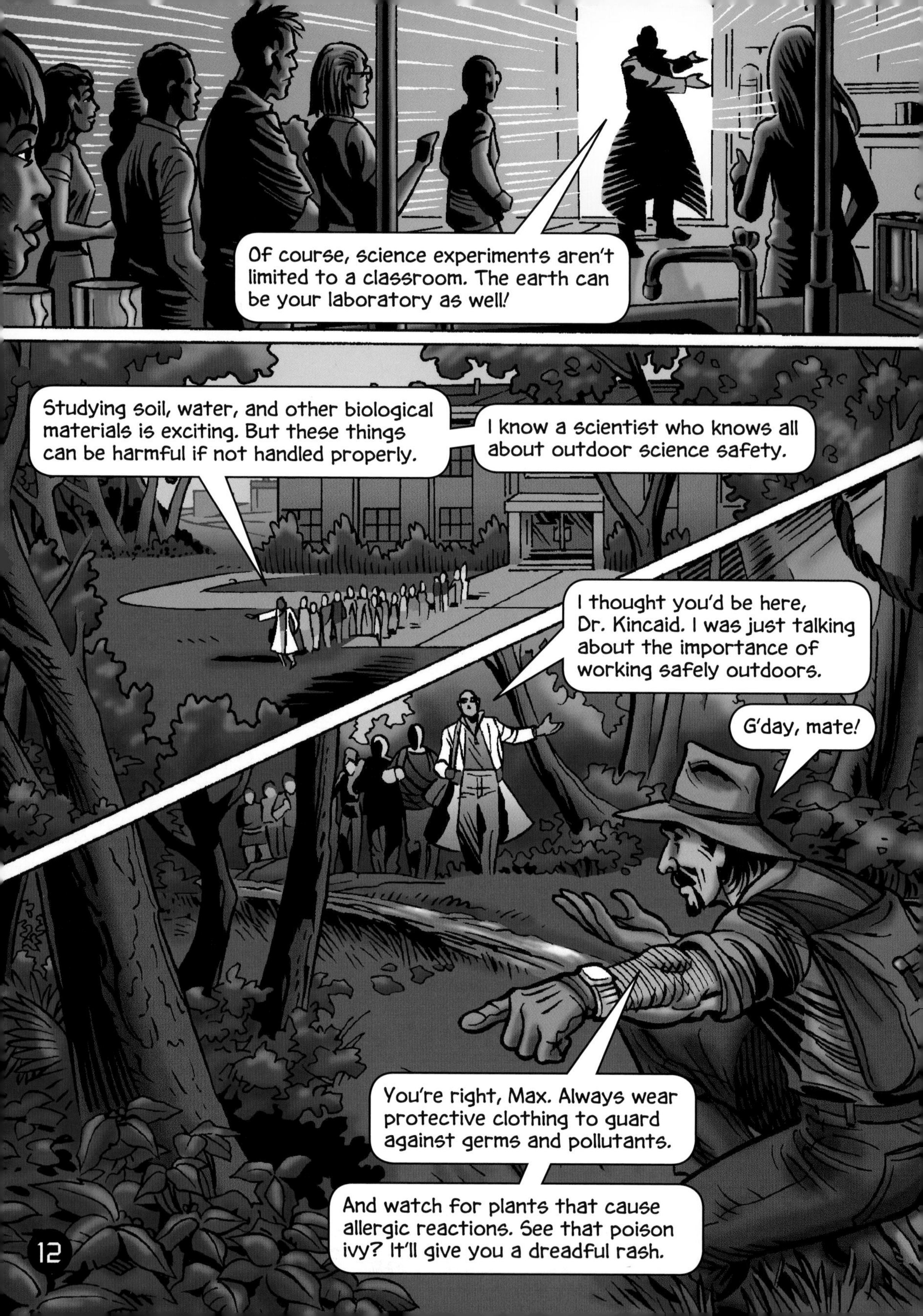
Of course, science experiments aren't limited to a classroom. The earth can be your laboratory as well!
Studying soil, water, and other biological materials is exciting. But these things can be harmful if not handled properly.
I know a scientist who knows all about outdoor science safety.
I thought you'd be here, Dr. Kincaid. I was just talking about the importance of working safely outdoors.
G'day, mate!
You're right, Max. Always wear protective clothing to guard against germs and pollutants.
And watch for plants that cause allergic reactions. See that poison ivy? It'll give you a dreadful rash.

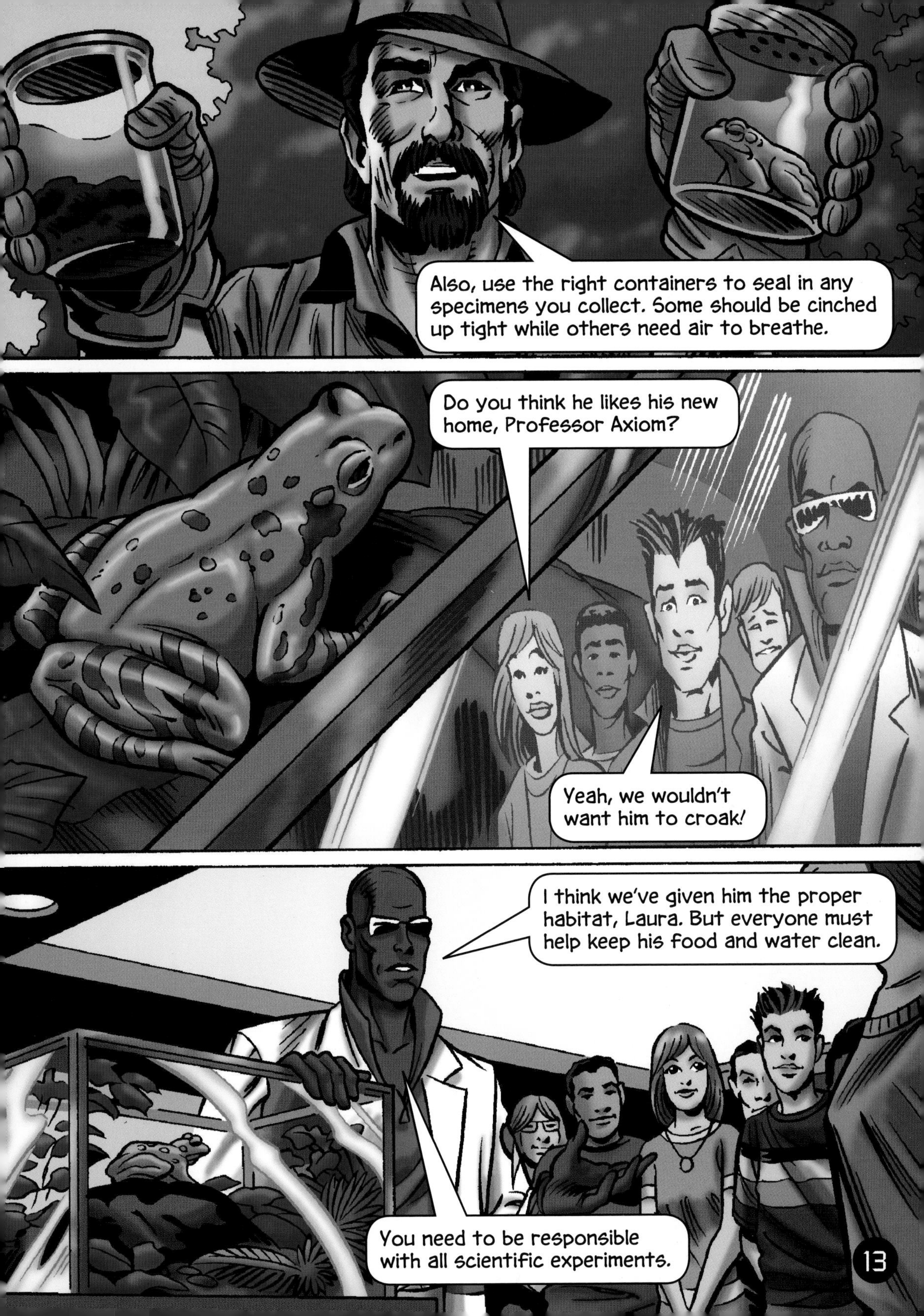
Also, use the right containers to seal in any specimens you collect. Some should be cinched up tight while others need air to breathe.
Do you think he likes his new home, Professor Axiom?
Yeah, we wouldn't want him to croak!
I think we've given him the proper habitat, Laura. But everyone must help keep his food and water clean.
You need to be responsible with all scientific experiments.

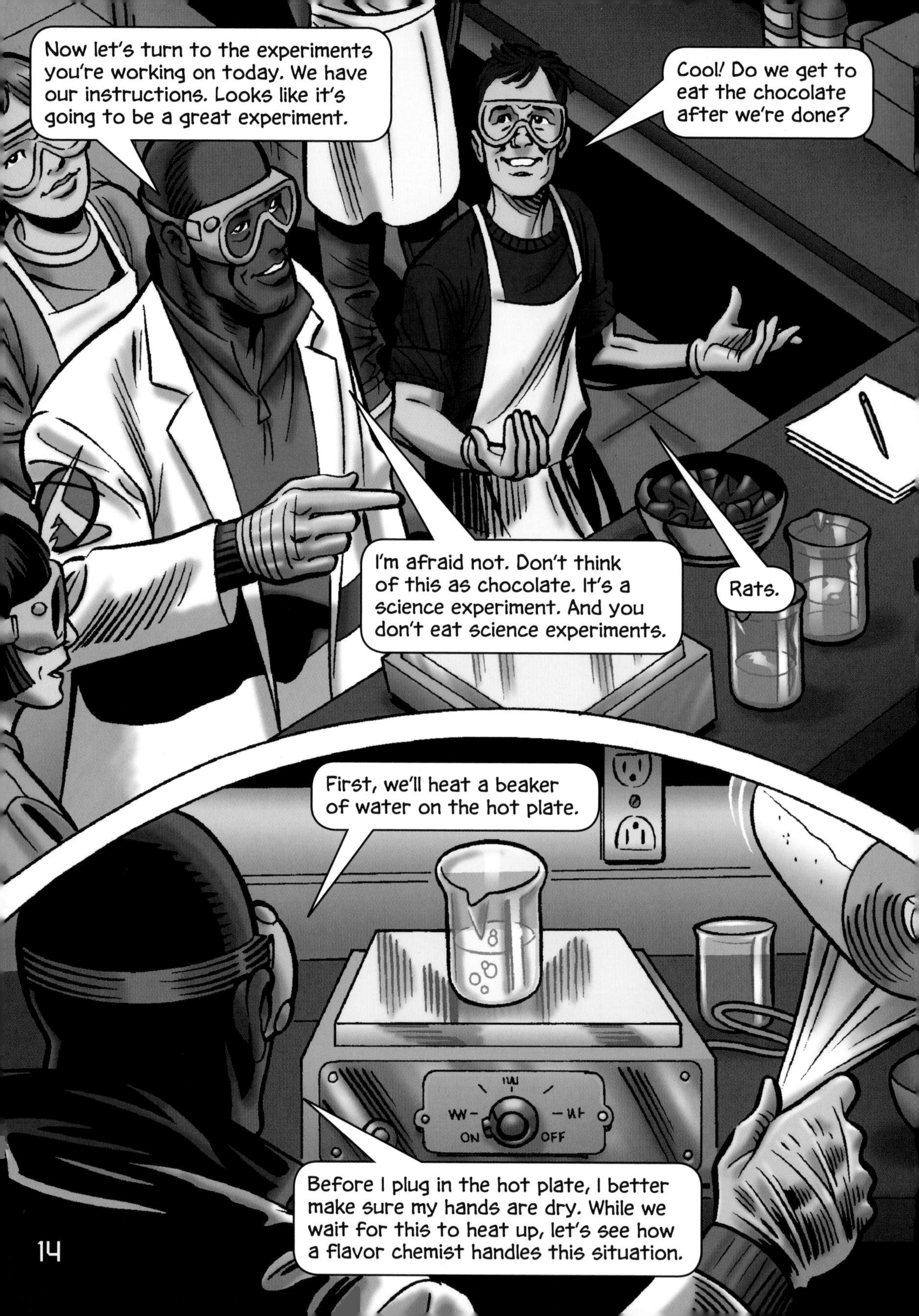
Now let's turn to the experiments you're working on today. We have our instructions. Looks like it's going to be a great experiment.
Cool! Do we get to eat the chocolate after we're done?
I'm afraid not. Don't think of this as chocolate. It's a science experiment. And you don't eat science experiments.
Rats.
First, we'll heat a beaker of water on the hot plate.
ON
OFF
Before I plug in the hot plate, I better make sure my hands are dry. While we wait for this to heat up, let's see how a flavor chemist handles this situation.

Dr. Lopez?

Hi, Max. I'm testing a sticky lollipop mixture.

I have to stay here and watch it heat up. We never leave a heat source unattended.

I'm testing different flavors to see how higher heat affects each one.

149° C

Just like Dr. Lopez, we're using glass beakers to heat our water and chocolate.

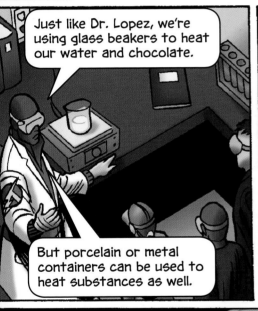

But porcelain or metal containers can be used to heat substances as well.

Whatever container is used, it should have a label that says "heat resistant."

HEAT RESISTANT

Looks like your water is ready for the next step in this experiment.

Professor Axiom!

Uh-oh. I better see what's going on over there.

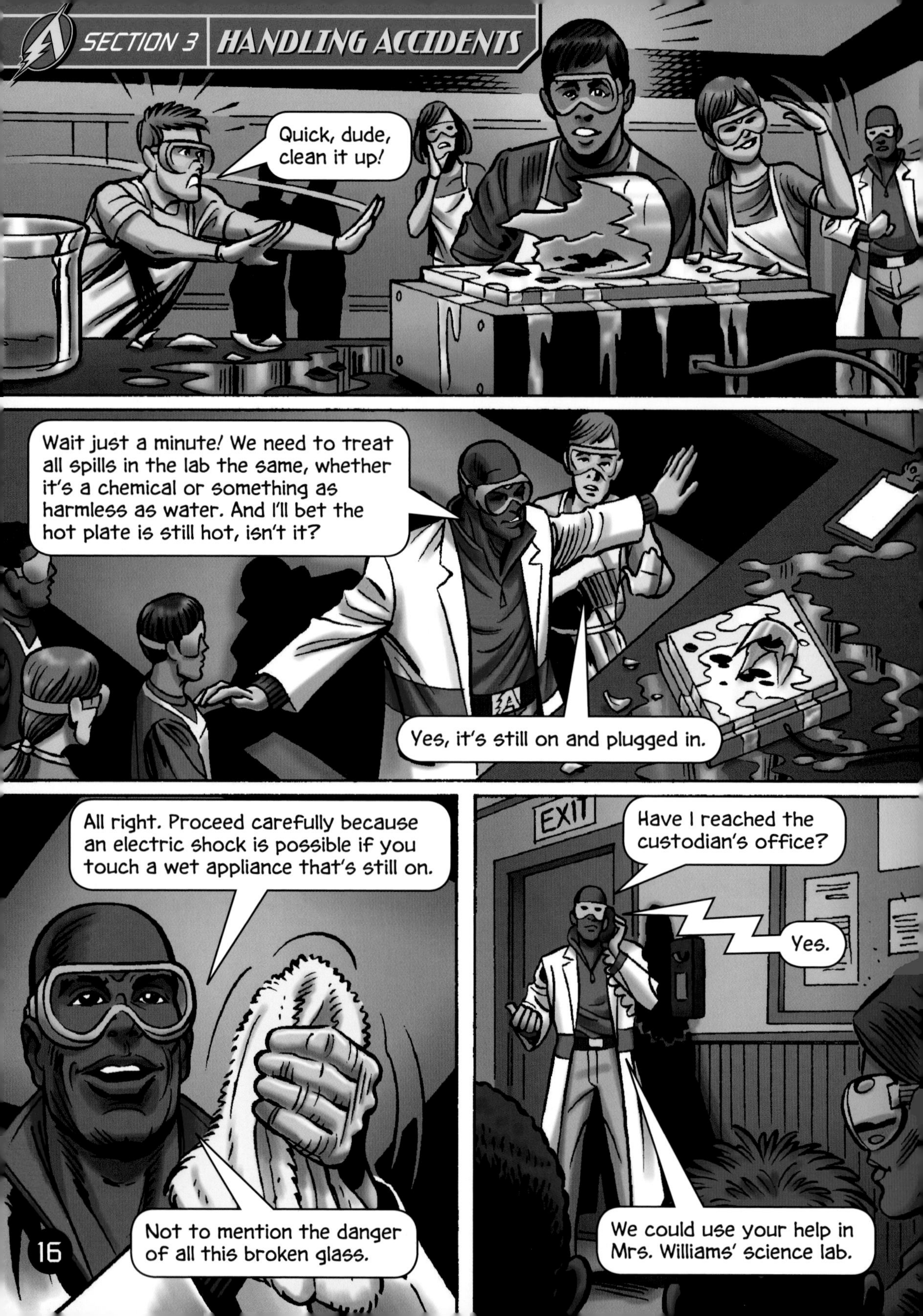
SECTION 3 HANDLING ACCIDENTS
Quick, dude, clean it up!
Wait just a minute! We need to treat all spills in the lab the same, whether it's a chemical or something as harmless as water. And I'll bet the hot plate is still hot, isn't it?
Yes, it's still on and plugged in.
All right. Proceed carefully because an electric shock is possible if you touch a wet appliance that's still on.
Not to mention the danger of all this broken glass.
EXIT
Have I reached the custodian's office?
Yes.
We could use your help in Mrs. Williams' science lab.
16

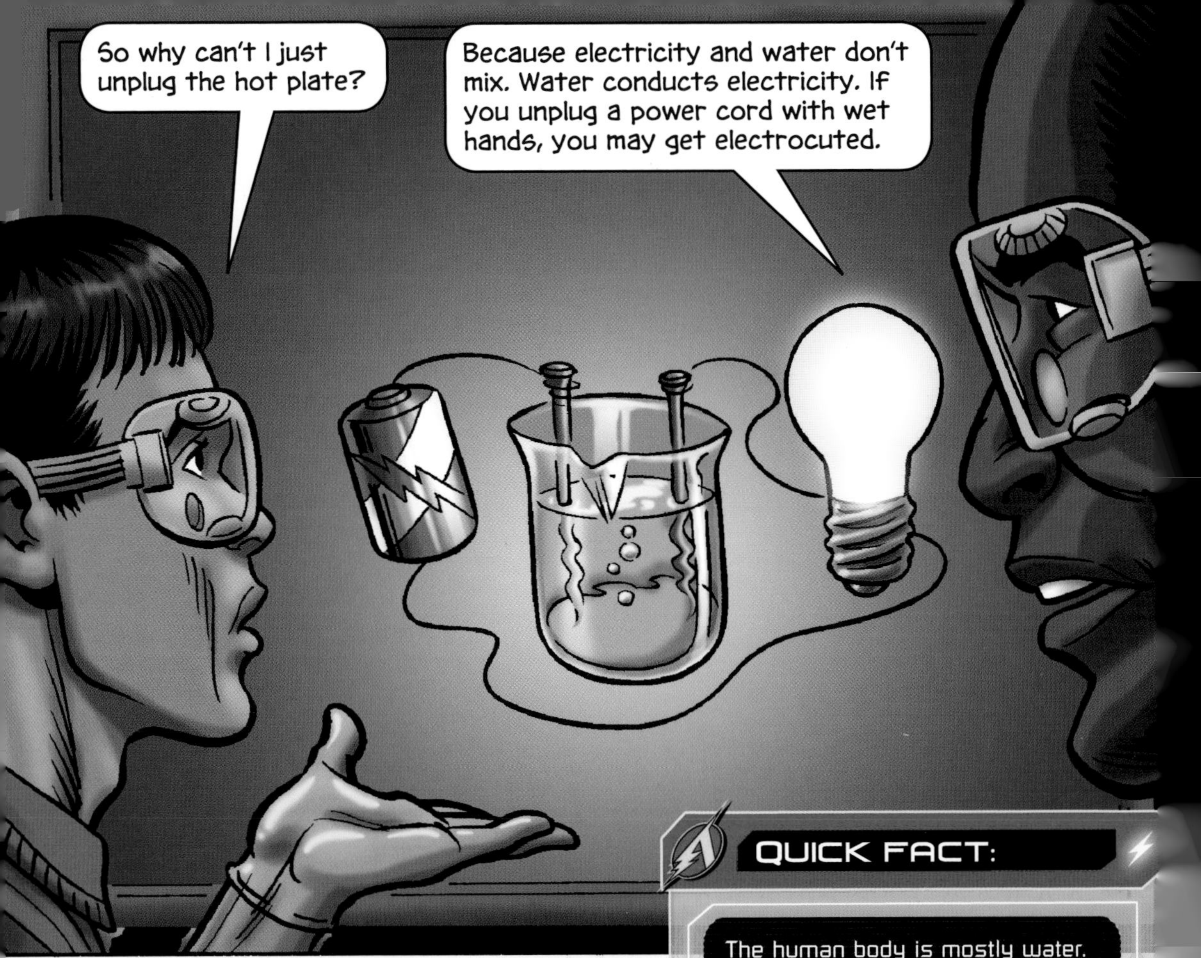
So why can't I just unplug the hot plate?
Because electricity and water don't mix. Water conducts electricity. If you unplug a power cord with wet hands, you may get electrocuted.

QUICK FACT:

The human body is mostly water. So your body conducts electricity. That's why you must be careful around electrical appliances.

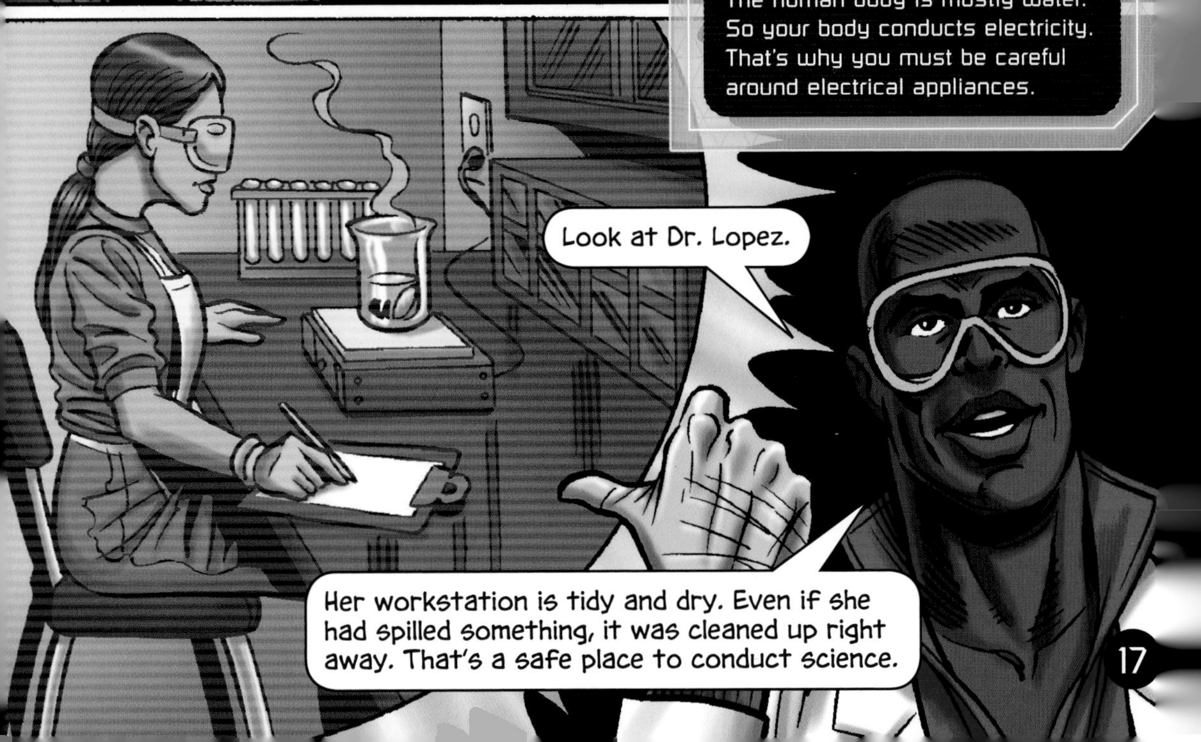
Look at Dr. Lopez.
Her workstation is tidy and dry. Even if she had spilled something, it was cleaned up right away. That's a safe place to conduct science.

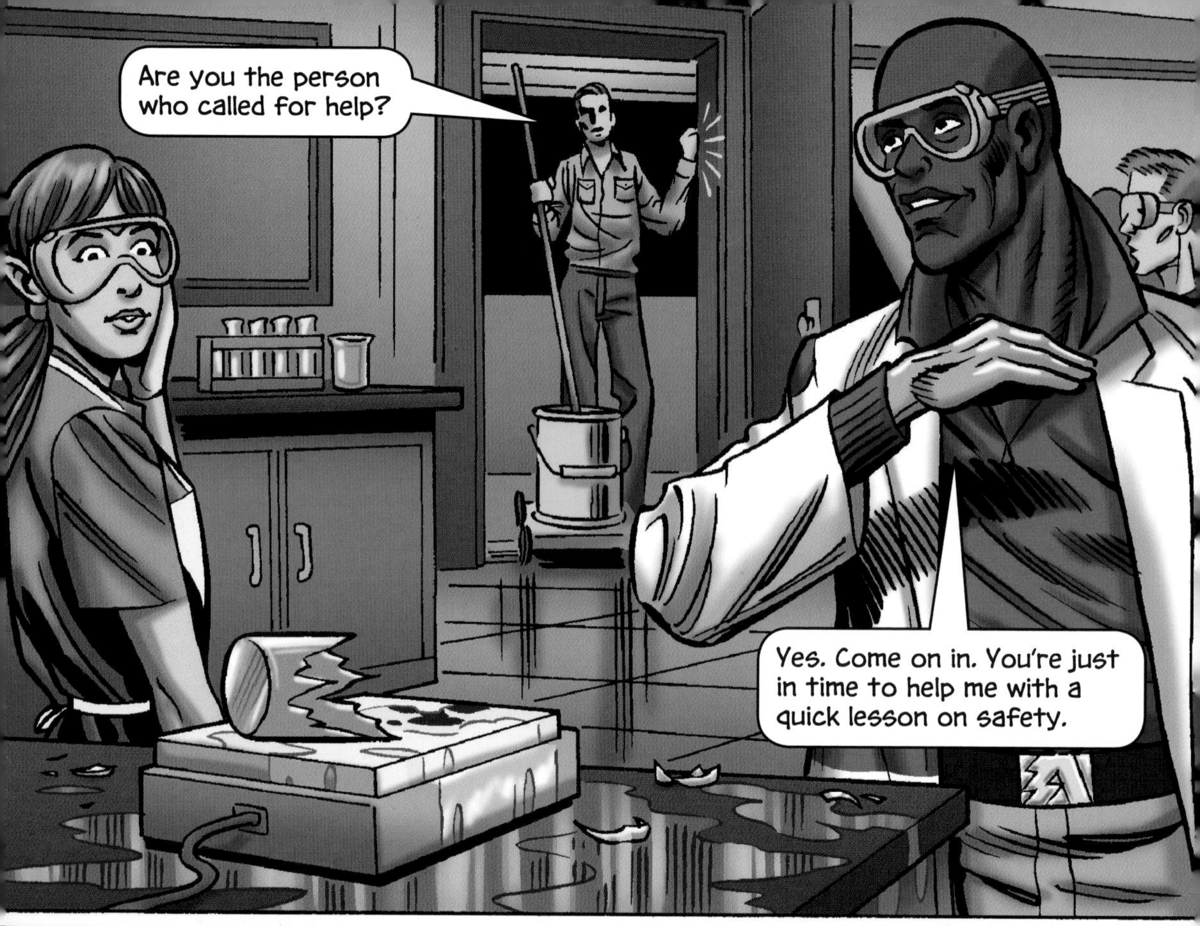
Are you the person who called for help?
Yes. Come on in. You're just in time to help me with a quick lesson on safety.

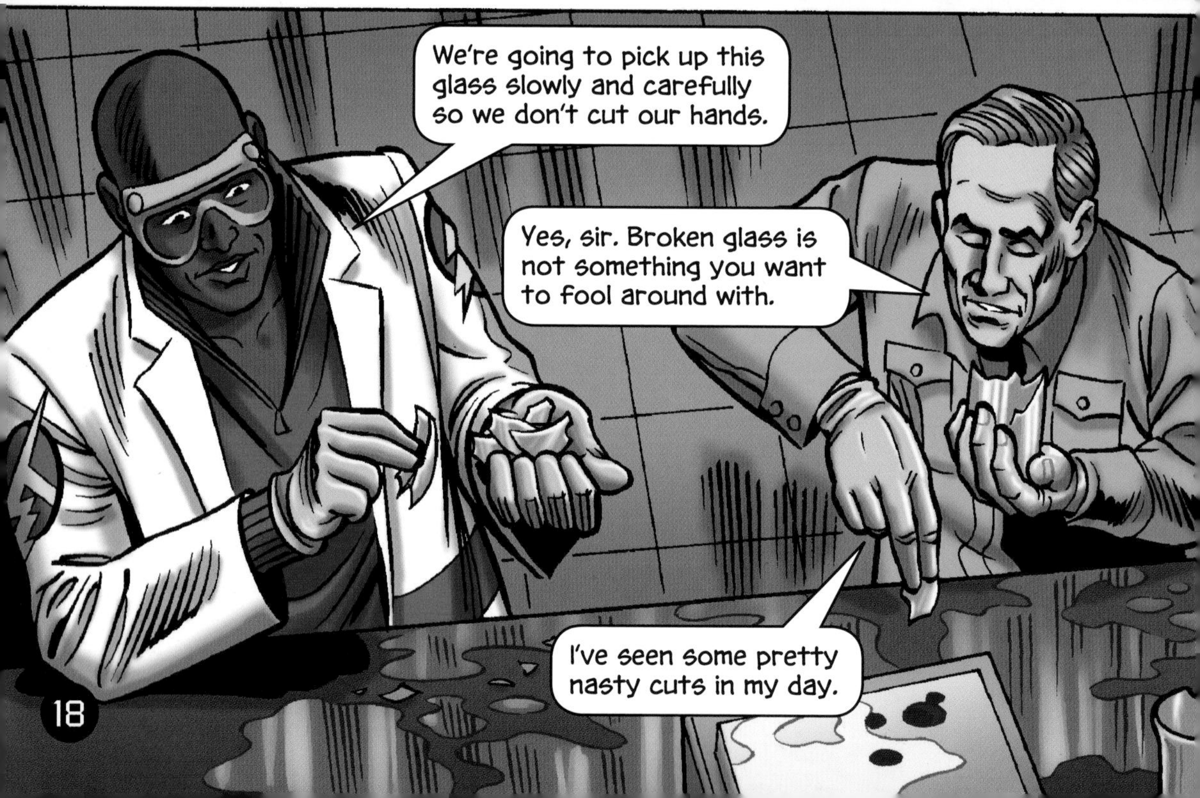
We're going to pick up this glass slowly and carefully so we don't cut our hands.
Yes, sir. Broken glass is not something you want to fool around with.
I've seen some pretty nasty cuts in my day.

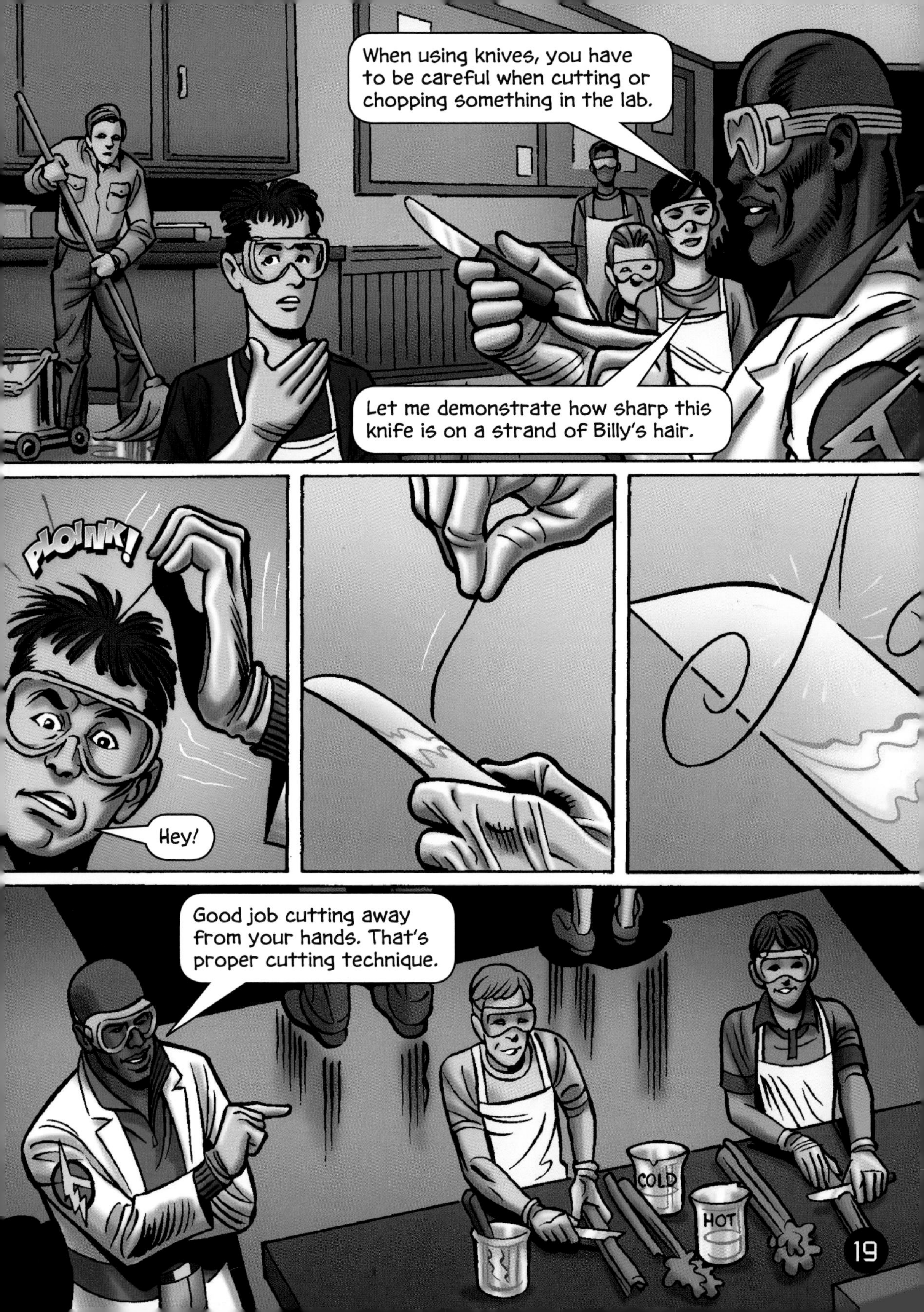
When using knives, you have to be careful when cutting or chopping something in the lab.
Let me demonstrate how sharp this knife is on a strand of Billy's hair.
PLOINK!
Hey!
Good job cutting away from your hands. That's proper cutting technique.
COLD
HOT

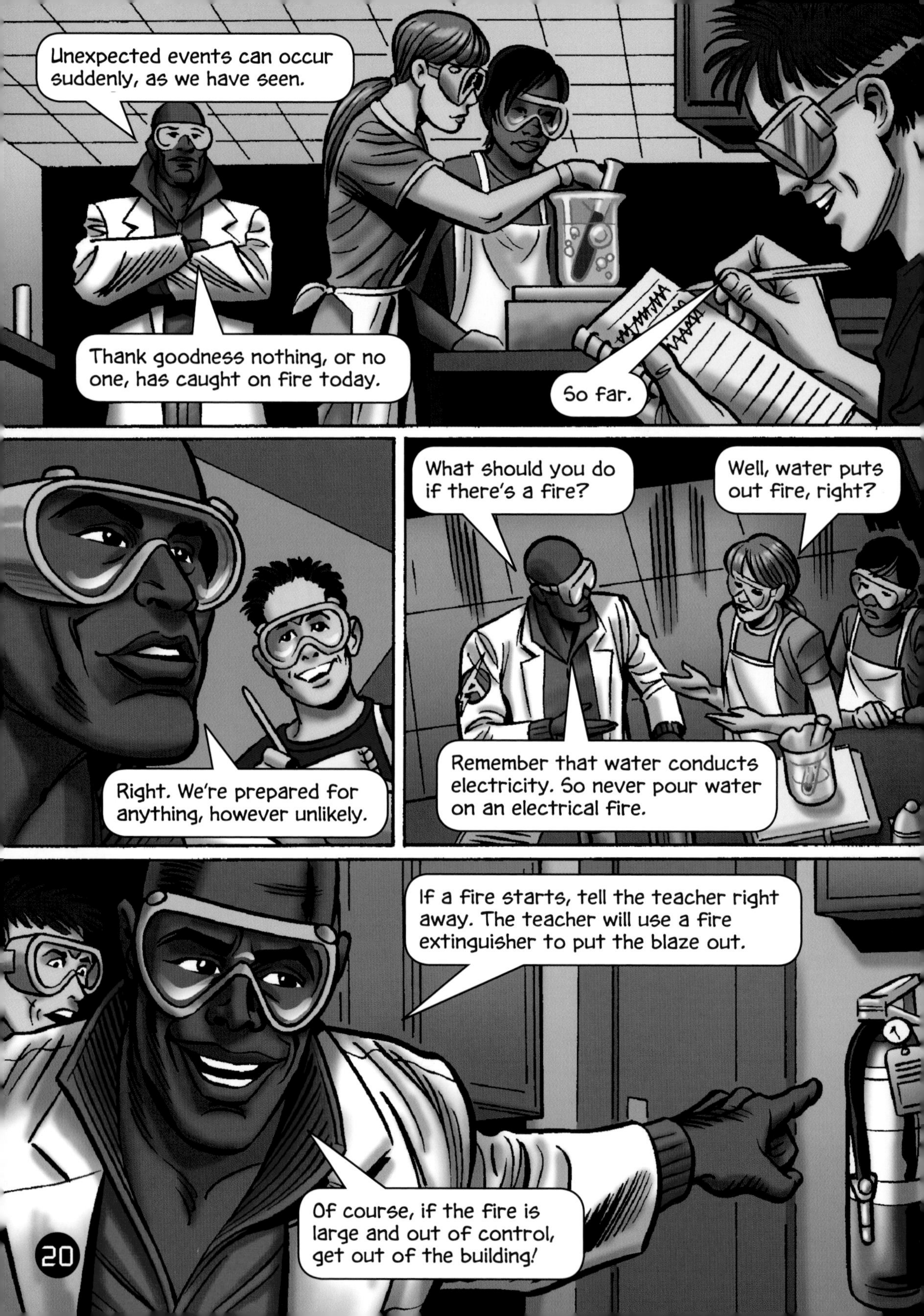
Unexpected events can occur suddenly, as we have seen.
Thank goodness nothing, or no one, has caught on fire today.
So far.
Right. We're prepared for anything, however unlikely.
What should you do if there's a fire?
Well, water puts out fire, right?
Remember that water conducts electricity. So never pour water on an electrical fire.
If a fire starts, tell the teacher right away. The teacher will use a fire extinguisher to put the blaze out.
Of course, if the fire is large and out of control, get out of the building!

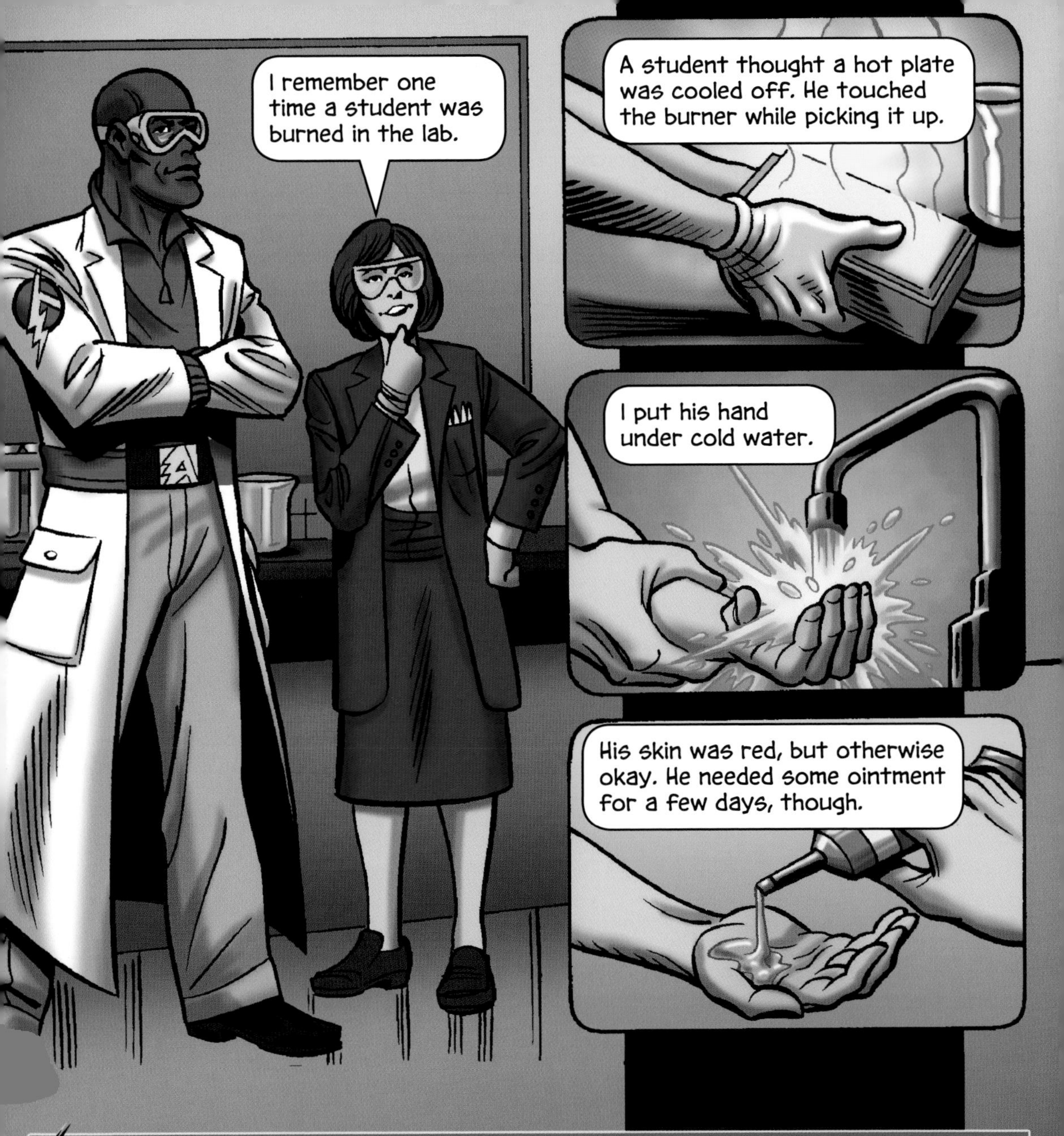
I remember one time a student was burned in the lab.
A student thought a hot plate was cooled off. He touched the burner while picking it up.
I put his hand under cold water.
His skin was red, but otherwise okay. He needed some ointment for a few days, though.

STOP, DROP, AND ROLL

ACCESS GRANTED: MAX AXIOM

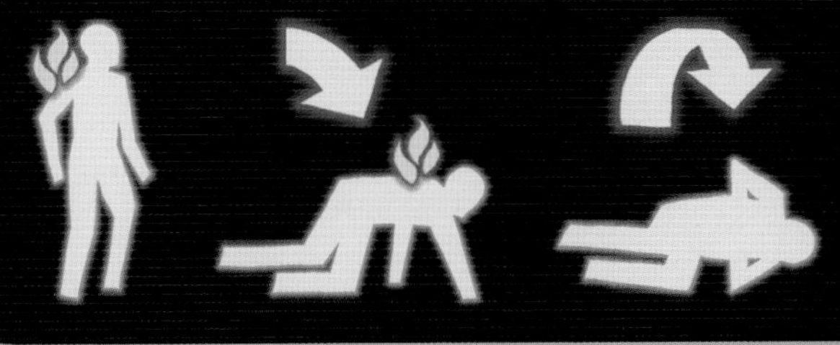

If your clothes catch fire, you need to put out the flames fast. Three simple steps can save your life. Stop what you are doing. Drop to the ground. Roll your body to smother the flames.

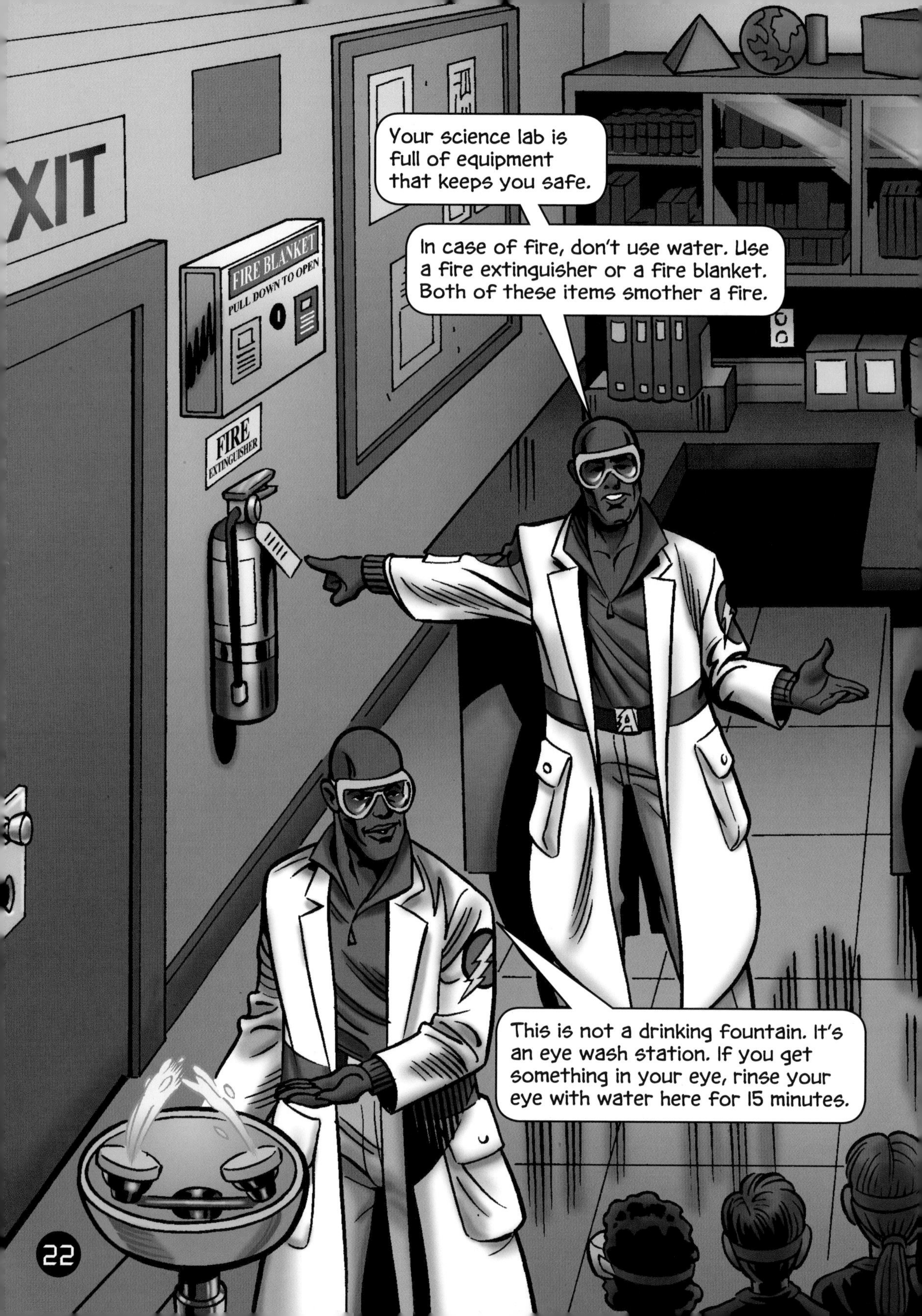
XIT
FIRE BLANKET
PULL DOWN TO OPEN
FIRE EXTINGUISHER
Your science lab is full of equipment that keeps you safe.
In case of fire, don't use water. Use a fire extinguisher or a fire blanket. Both of these items smother a fire.
This is not a drinking fountain. It's an eye wash station. If you get something in your eye, rinse your eye with water here for 15 minutes.

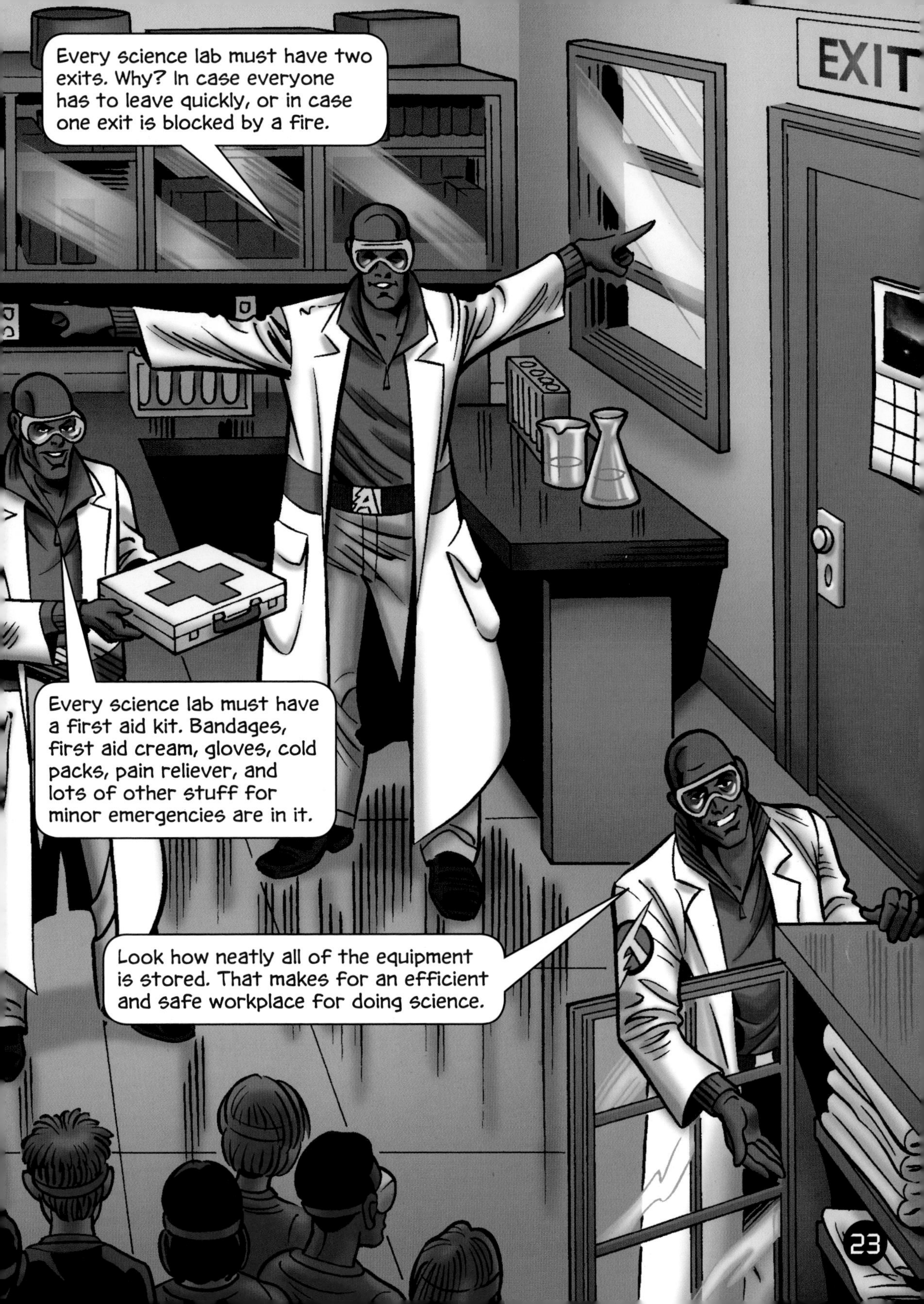
EXIT
Every science lab must have two exits. Why? In case everyone has to leave quickly, or in case one exit is blocked by a fire.
Every science lab must have a first aid kit. Bandages, first aid cream, gloves, cold packs, pain reliever, and lots of other stuff for minor emergencies are in it.
Look how neatly all of the equipment is stored. That makes for an efficient and safe workplace for doing science.

SECTION 4 CLEANING UP

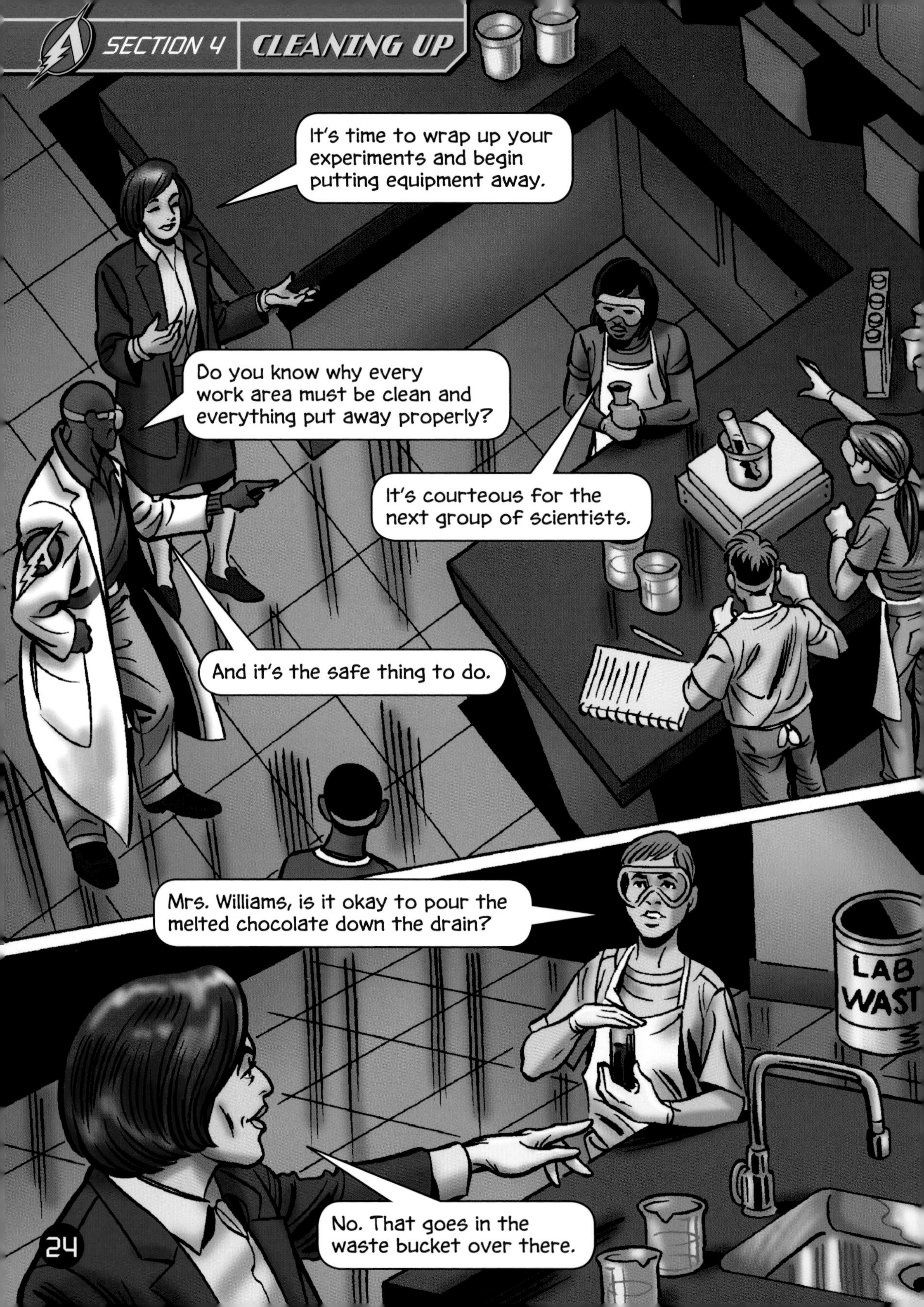

It's time to wrap up your experiments and begin putting equipment away.
Do you know why every work area must be clean and everything put away properly?
It's courteous for the next group of scientists.
And it's the safe thing to do.
Mrs. Williams, is it okay to pour the melted chocolate down the drain?
LAB WAST
No. That goes in the waste bucket over there.

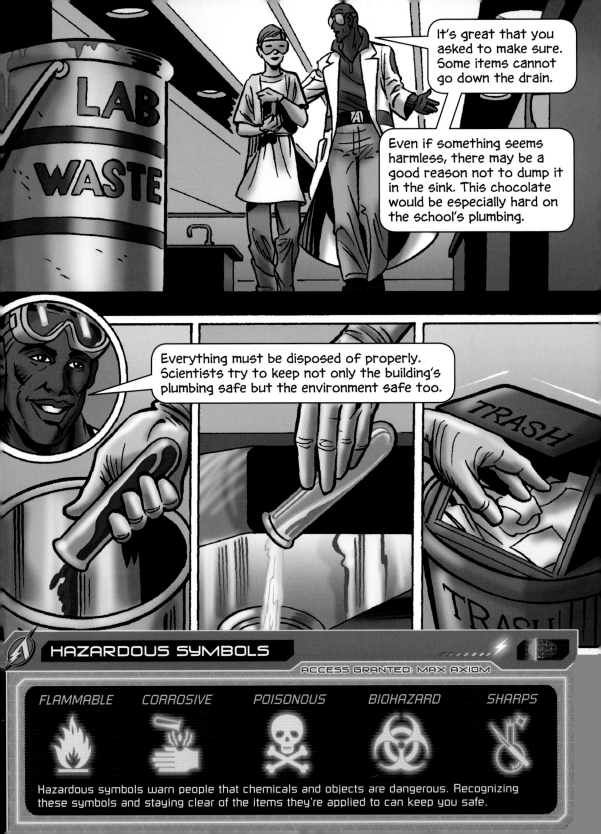

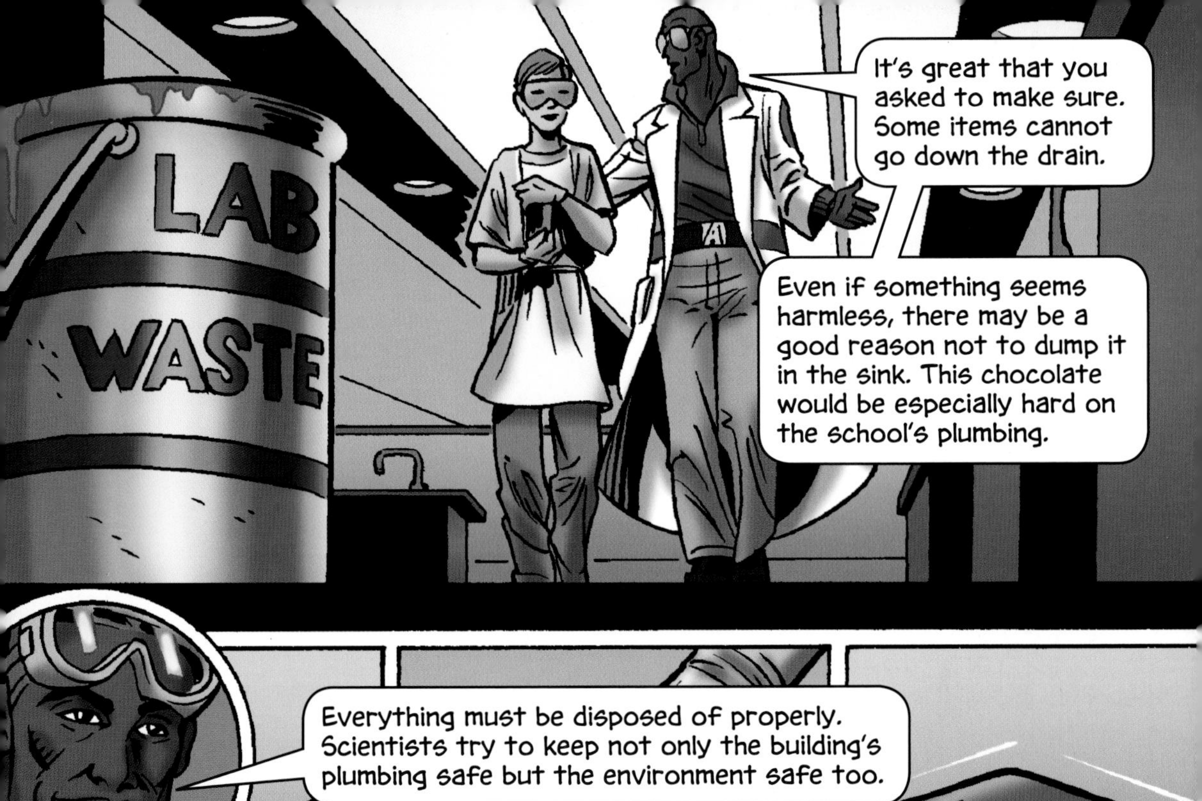
LAB
WASTE
It's great that you asked to make sure. Some items cannot go down the drain.
Even if something seems harmless, there may be a good reason not to dump it in the sink. This chocolate would be especially hard on the school's plumbing.
Everything must be disposed of properly. Scientists try to keep not only the building's plumbing safe but the environment safe too.
TRASH

HAZARDOUS SYMBOLS

ACCESS GRANTED: MAX AXIOM

FLAMMABLE *CORROSIVE* *POISONOUS* *BIOHAZARD* *SHARPS*

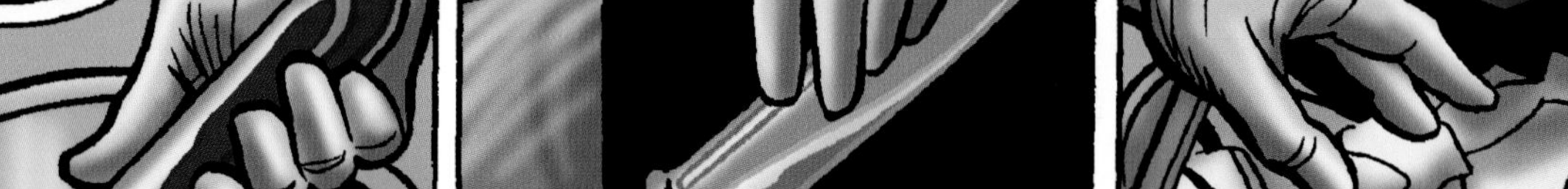

Hazardous symbols warn people that chemicals and objects are dangerous. Recognizing these symbols and staying clear of the items they're applied to can keep you safe.

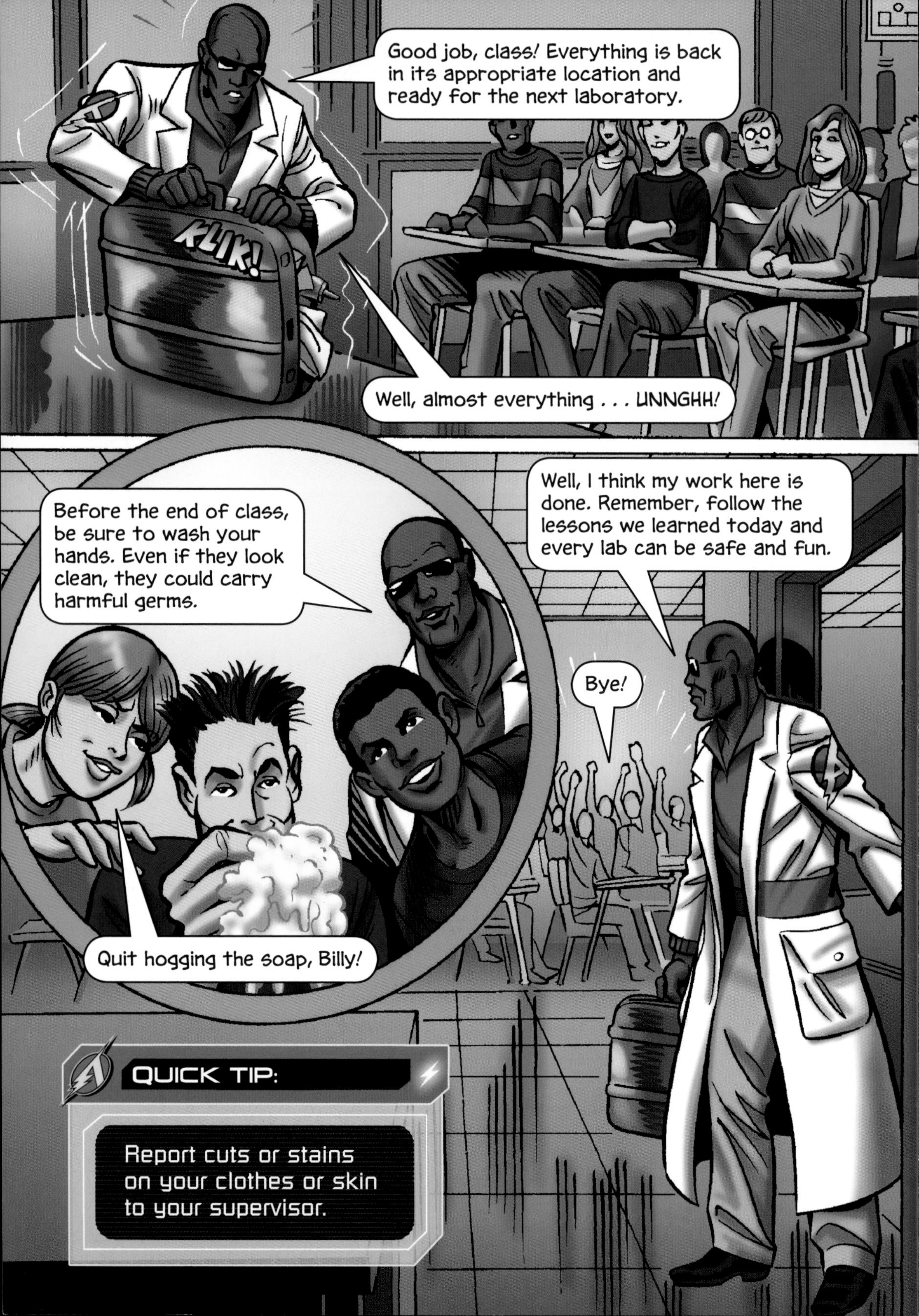
Good job, class! Everything is back in its appropriate location and ready for the next laboratory.
KLIK!
Well, almost everything . . . UNNGHH!
Before the end of class, be sure to wash your hands. Even if they look clean, they could carry harmful germs.
Quit hogging the soap, Billy!
Well, I think my work here is done. Remember, follow the lessons we learned today and every lab can be safe and fun.
Bye!
QUICK TIP:
Report cuts or stains on your clothes or skin to your supervisor.

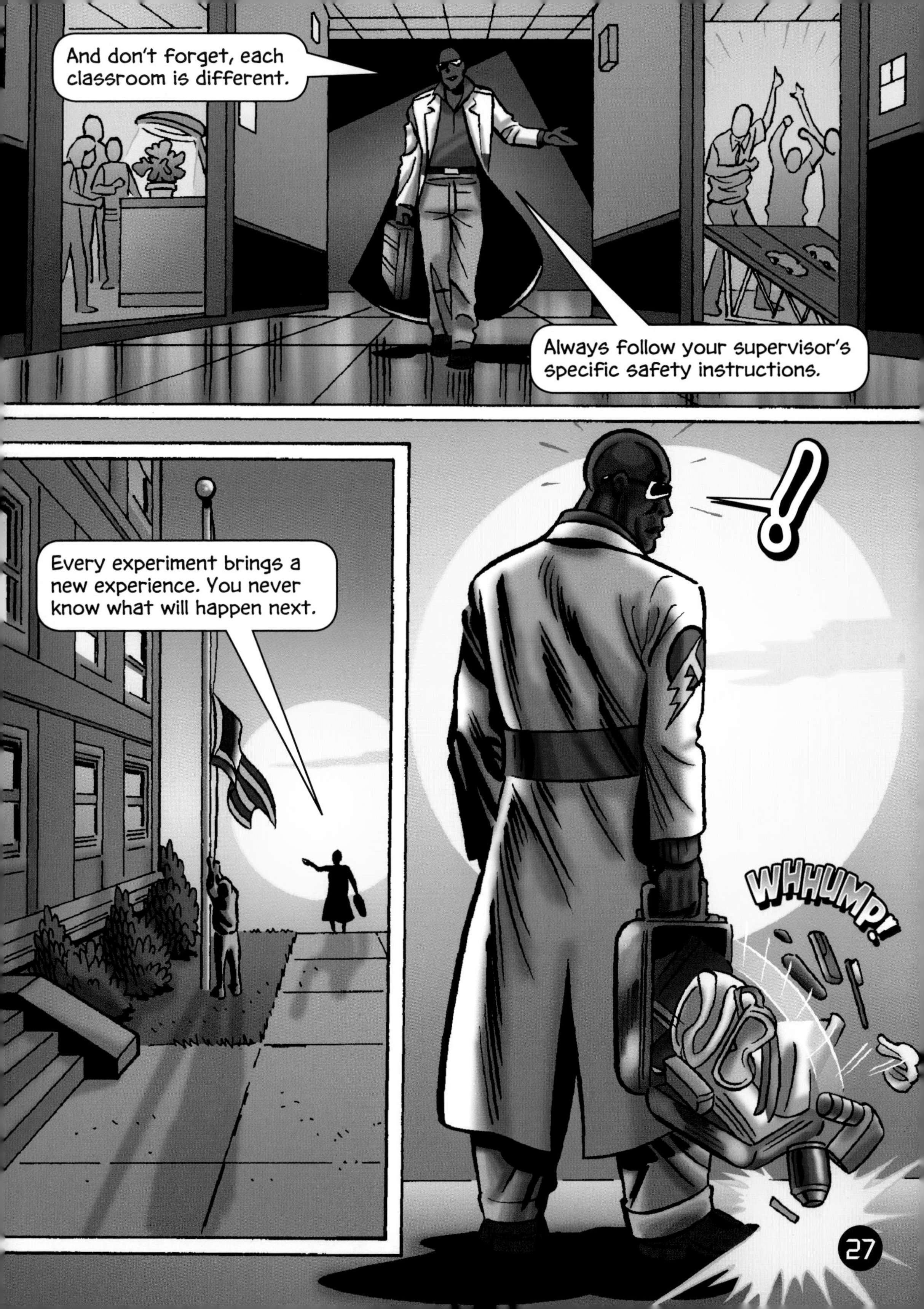
And don't forget, each classroom is different.
Always follow your supervisor's specific safety instructions.
Every experiment brings a new experience. You never know what will happen next.
!
WHHUMP!

SCIENCE SAFETY

Before beginning a lab experiment, be sure you understand the instructions completely. If your teacher explains the instructions, listen closely. Ask questions if you don't understand. If the instructions are written, read them carefully and follow each step exactly. If you have any questions during the experiment, ask your teacher.

They may not be fashionable, but safety goggles must be worn at all times in the lab. For the best protection, use goggles that shield your eyes from both chemical splashes and flying objects. These goggles are always labeled with the code ANSI Z87.1.

Right now your body has more germs on it than there are people living in the United States! Washing your hands for at least 20 seconds is the best way to prevent millions of germs from passing to your mouth, nose, and eyes.

Environmental scientists test soil and water for pollutants. In 1989, the *Exxon Valdez* crashed and spilled oil into Prince William Sound, Alaska. Wearing protective clothing, environmental scientists helped determine the best cleanup methods. With their help, the area is slowly returning to a healthy environment.

Learning about animals is fun, but handle lab animals only if your teacher gives you permission. If a lab animal bites or scratches you, be sure to tell your teacher immediately. Also, wash your hands before and after you handle an animal. Washing hands protects you from passing germs to or receiving germs from the animal.

Scientists use safety equipment for the type of science they are doing. Scientists studying erupting volcanoes sometimes wear silver full-body suits. These suits have a metal coating that reflects the intense heat of molten lava. Scientists studying sharks sometimes wear shark suits when diving. These suits are made of a steel mesh that protects against shark bites.

 Some protective gloves are made of latex. This material can cause an allergic reaction in some people. If you experience a rash or itching while wearing latex gloves, tell your supervisor.

MORE ABOUT

SUPER SCIENTIST

Real name: Maxwell J. Axiom
Hometown: Seattle, Washington
Height: 6' 1"   **Weight:** 192 lbs
Eyes: Brown   **Hair:** None

Super capabilities: Super intelligence; able to shrink to the size of an atom; sunglasses give x-ray vision; lab coat allows for travel through time and space.

Origin: Since birth, Max Axiom seemed destined for greatness. His mother, a marine biologist, taught her son about the mysteries of the sea. His father, a nuclear physicist and volunteer park ranger, schooled Max on the wonders of earth and sky.

One day on a wilderness hike, a megacharged lightning bolt struck Max with blinding fury. When he awoke, Max discovered a newfound energy and set out to learn as much about science as possible. He traveled the globe earning degrees in every aspect of the field. Upon his return, he was ready to share his knowledge and new identity with the world. He had become Max Axiom, Super Scientist.

GLOSSARY

allergic reaction (uh-LUR-jik ree-AK-shuhn)—sneezing, watery eyes, swelling, or rashes caused by contact with plants, animals, or substances

biohazard (BYE-oh-haz-urd)—a biological agent, such as blood or body fluids, that may carry infectious diseases

biologist (bye-OL-uh-jist)—a scientist who studies living things

chemist (KEM-ist)—a scientist who studies or works with chemicals

contaminated (kuhn-TAM-uh-nay-tid)—dirty or unfit for use

corrosive (kuh-ROW-siv)—able to destroy or eat away at something little by little

flammable (FLAM-uh-buhl)—able to burn

germs (JURMS)—small living things that cause disease; bacteria and viruses are two common types of germs.

habitat (HAB-uh-tat)—the place and natural conditions where an animal lives

latex (LAY-teks)—a milky liquid that comes from certain plants; latex is used to make rubber.

poisonous (POI-zuhn-uhss)—able to kill or harm if swallowed, inhaled, or touched

porcelain (POR-suh-lin)—a hard ceramic made by firing and glazing clay

sharps (SHARPS)—knives, needles, and broken glass

specimen (SPESS-uh-muhn)—a sample that a scientist studies closely

READ MORE

Bender, Lionel. *Science Safety: Being Careful.* Amazing Science. Minneapolis: Picture Window Books, 2007.

Burke, Melissa Blackwell. *Think Like a Scientist.* Pair-It Books. Austin, Texas: Steck-Vaughn, 2000.

Churchill, E. Richard. Amazing Science Experiments. No Sweat Science. New York: Sterling, 2005.

Henderson, Joyce, and Heather Tomasello. *So You Have to Do a Science Fair Project.* New York: Wiley, 2002.

Pederson, Bridget. *Don't Be Hasty with Science Safety!* Science Made Simple. Edina, Minn.: Abdo, 2007.

Richardson, Adele. *Electricity: A Question and Answer Book.* Questions and Answers: Physical Science. Mankato, Minn.: Capstone Press, 2006.

INTERNET SITES

FactHound offers a safe, fun way to find Internet sites related to this book. All of the sites on FactHound have been researched by our staff.

Here's how:
1. Visit *www.facthound.com*
2. Choose your grade level.
3. Type in this book ID **0736868348** for age-appropriate sites. You may also browse subjects by clicking on letters, or by clicking on pictures and words.
4. Click on the **Fetch It** button.

FactHound will fetch the best sites for you!

INDEX

accidents, 6, 8, 16–23, 26
    broken glass, 16, 18
    burns, 21
    fires, 20, 21, 22
    spills, 6, 16
allergies, 12, 29
animals, 13, 28
asking questions, 5, 28

beakers, 10, 14, 15
biological materials,
    12–13, 28

chemicals, 10–11, 16, 25, 28
cleaning up, 24–25

electricity, 16, 17, 20
emergencies, 5, 23
exits, 23
experiments, 5, 8, 10, 11, 12,
    13, 14, 15, 24, 27, 28

food and beverages, 8–9
fumes, 11

germs, 6, 7, 9, 12, 26, 28

hazardous symbols, 25
heat resistant containers, 15
hot plates, 14–15, 16, 17, 21

instructions, 5, 8, 10, 14,
    27, 28

knives, 19

labeling containers, 11
lab waste, 24–25

pollutants, 12, 28
protective clothing, 6–7, 8,
    12, 28, 29

rules, 5

safety equipment
    aprons, 6
    eye wash stations, 22
    fire blankets, 22
    fire extinguishers, 20, 22
    first aid kits, 23
    gloves, 6, 23, 29
    goggles, 6, 28
sharps, 18–19, 25
stop, drop, and roll, 21

tidy workstations, 8–9, 17, 24

wafting, 11
washing hands, 26, 28